HOW WELL DO YOU KNOW THE MOFFATTS?

What was Scott's most embarrassing moment?
Do you know Dave's favorite food?
Can you name Clint's favorite band?
What's Bob's favorite movie?
How did the band get their start?

FIND OUT THE ANSWERS— AND A WHOLE LOT MORE—IN THE MOFFATTS

*St. Martin's Paperbacks Titles
by Anna Louise Golden*

'N SYNC

FIVE

BRANDY

BACKSTREET BOYS

THE MOFFATTS

Anna Louise Golden

St. Martin's Paperbacks

NOTE: If you purchased this book without a cover you should be aware that this book is stolen property. It was reported as "unsold and destroyed" to the publisher, and neither the author nor the publisher has received any payment for this "stripped book."

THE MOFFATTS

Copyright © 1999 by Anna Louise Golden.
Cover photograph © Warren Johnson/Rex USA Ltd.

All rights reserved. No part of this book may be used or reproduced in any manner whatsoever without written permission except in the case of brief quotations embodied in critical articles or reviews. For information address St. Martin's Press, 175 Fifth Avenue, New York, NY 10010.

ISBN: 0-312-97359-4

Printed in the United States of America

St. Martin's Paperbacks edition / August 1999

10 9 8 7 6 5 4 3 2 1

Acknowledgments

It might be my name on the cover, but any book is the work of many people. Always the first to thank is my marvelous agent, Madeleine Morel, without whom ... well, I don't want to think about it. And there's Glenda Howard, my editor, with whom it's always a pleasure to work, and also the rest of the team at St. Martin's Press, from legal to copyedit and beyond. Thank you. My mum and dad have offered constant encouragement, not just on this project, but throughout my life. Friends in England and America are supportive, and very understanding when I'm too tired from work to go out. And then there are L&G ... my heartbeats. Suffice to say that no girl works alone. . . .

I'm grateful, too, to articles that have appeared in *Bop, Tiger Beat, Bravo, Popcorn, Megastar, MAX, All-Stars, Winnipeg Free Press* (by Bartley Kives, July 28, 1998), *The Canadian Press, Toronto Star, Pop Rocky, Maclean's, Teen People, The Manila Times, Hit Sensations,* and *Teenbeat*.

Introduction

You already know it, but just in case there's any doubt about the matter—the Moffatts are a rock band. They used to be a country group—that was how they made their name—but they grew up and reinvented themselves, found what they loved and went with it. People have accused them of simply cashing in on the Hanson trend, but that's very far from the case. Do you still love the same things you did five years ago? Probably not. Tastes change. And by the time Hanson started putting out records, the Moffatts (or the Moffatt Brothers, as they were once known) already had two albums out, and Hanson acknowledged them as an influence!

The four Canadian siblings—Scott, and triplets, Bob, Dave, and Clint—have been singing for a full decade now, not too shabby when you consider that Scott is just sixteen and the other three a year younger. They've grown up in music, guided by their father Frank, who spent a lot of his own youth singing in rock bands, their mother Darlana, who was named one of the top Canadian jazz vocalists in 1978, and, more recently, their stepmother, Sheila. It's not too often you'll find four brothers who are so close to each other (of course, it's not *that* often you'll find triplets, really).

They've come a long way from the trip to Alberta's West Edmonton Mall, where the brothers made their own record, a cover of the Judds' "Grandpa (Tell Me 'Bout The Good Ole Days)," which they really *were* recording for their grandparents, to being the hottest teen act around, and quite definitely the biggest thing out of Canada since Alanis Morrissette. Along the way they just happened to be the youngest country group ever to sign with a major U.S. record label, after being nominated for five awards from the British Columbia Country Music Association and finishing a forty-date (!) Canadian tour—by which time Scott was all of eight years old! In 1994, after stints in Branson, Missouri, and Las Vegas, they relocated from their home in Victoria to Nashville, Tennessee, Music City USA itself, the center of country music, touring all over, appearing regularly on TNN and TNT, learning music, and how to play their instruments. Scott proved to be a natural on guitar, and the others fell in line, Clint on bass, Bob on the drums, and Dave on the keyboards.

Growing up in public hasn't been easy. There's been a lot of time on the road, a lot of home schooling (courtesy of their father), and not the chance to really enjoy a childhood. On the plus side, though, how many kids their age have gotten to see so much of the world? And how many have had the chance to entertain audiences all over—in Canada, Europe, Asia, and the U.S.?

Around the globe, they've had records going gold and platinum, no small feat for anyone. They've even been responsible for a country line-dance, the Caterpillar Crawl, which they invented in the mid-Nineties—and which is now preserved on record and video, although you might find it difficult to get hold of the video, since it's out of print these days.

But changing the music they played has proved to be a very big deal indeed, and it's what's really catapulted them to international stardom, although America is only just beginning to catch up with the phenomenon. When they were younger, country suited the Moffatts; it was a kind of music kids could comfortably sing. But as they grew up, and started being more aware of what they really wanted, rock seemed the only way to go for them.

"It's just a taste," Scott explains. "Teenagers get some aggression, they want rock music. We just wanted to play what we feel." What they feel, though, is still a little influenced by the gentler sounds of country, and also by bands like the Beatles, whom they all love (in performance they've been know to cover the Beatles' "She Loves You"). Bob might be a Metallica fan, and they might get into Bush and Nirvana, but there's no metal, grunge, or punk in their sound. "We play pop-rock so we can be more open to other kinds of music, too. If you play country you're country forever." And the Moffatts know they're still too young to commit to one kind of music forever. Besides, they're wise enough to know that a career in music is one long journey of discovery.

"We won't always be doing stuff like this," Scott says. "Our tastes change all the time—we're always finding new music styles."

They followed their hearts, but it's proved to have a very positive side effect. They were popular before, at least in country circles. But country circles are limited. Country fans like country, and not much else. People who are into pop and rock generally aren't into country. So, while it was a kind of rebirth for the band, it also introduced them to a new audience, one that was much bigger, much younger, and much more international than any they'd known when they were just singing and playing country music.

In 1997 they took themselves off to Germany, of all places, to do a lot of playing, rehearsing, and recording. While they were living there, the first single by the "new" Moffatts, "I'll Be There for You," climbed high up the German charts, even as they honed their music in the small town of Strommeln, outside Cologne, some four thousand miles from Nashville (and another couple of thousand miles from their real home on Canada's west coast). They took it all very seriously, playing from nine A.M. to two P.M. every day, going over and over their own material, improving their performances, even learning other people's songs, like a version of the Police's "Every Breath You Take."

It all took discipline, which was something Frank had instilled in his sons from a young age, and a lot of desire to succeed in this brand-new field. And it paid off big-time. Within a year they were more than another North American band playing in Germany. They'd proved just how cool they could be in Europe and in Asia—they drew an amazing *ten thousand* fans when they played a mall in Malaysia, a place where they also issued a special album, and found their CD, *Chapter 1: A New Beginning* (a very apt title, given the way they've reinvented themselves), going double platinum. For a new beginning, it couldn't have gone any better.

In the Philippines it was just as crazy. When they toured there last year—three times in the space of five months—they went from being complete unknowns to massive headliners. They started off by playing in the malls, and by their third visit they were headlining at the Big Dome in Manila while thousands of girls screamed for them. If that wasn't advancing rapidly, nothing was.

Essentially, it just repeated what had happened elsewhere. After *Chapter 1: A New Beginning*, their native Canada had gone crazy for them all over again. They totally disrupted a mall in Winnipeg when they played there, much to the delight of fans (and disgust of store owners, who were worried about teenage shoplifters, and also annoyed that the mall was so jammed that no one could get in their stores), playing for forty-five minutes, then sticking around for another two hours to sign autographs and chat with the kids who'd traveled to see them.

Clint, Dave, Bob, and Scott understand that it's the fans who are letting them reinvent themselves in this way, and who are accepting them. They've been in the music business—and don't ever be fooled; glamorous as it might seem at times, music really is a business—for a long time. They know the ins and outs, and they're very dedicated professionals. Even when they're out on the road, playing shows every night, they still rehearse and practice a couple of hours every day. When they're at home, that amount goes up to five or six hours. Now that's real dedication! Still, that's what you need. Their inspirations might have changed, from people like Garth Brooks to Nirvana and the Beatles, but the bottom line is they still work to make it all happen.

And now, finally, they're taking on the United States. They earned quite a reputation when they were a country act, the little sweethearts of Nashville, and the first order of business is to shake that off and be taken at face value, for who they are nowadays. It helps that most of the people who'll be listening to them as a pop band probably aren't even aware they ever sang country—to these fans they've just come out of nowhere, and in some ways that's a plus.

Having a song prominently featured on the soundtrack of the Drew Barrymore film, *Never Been Kissed*, is a good step, especially since the film is aimed squarely at the Moffatts' main audience—teens. That song, and a single, will pave the way for the American release of *Chapter 1: A New Beginning*, which will have four songs not available elsewhere in the world, co-written and produced by Glen Ballard, the man who helped transform Alanis from a Canadian teen queen into a serious artist, and who's also worked with Aerosmith, Michael Jackson, and any number of other acts. In other words, this is the very big time indeed. It's a certainty that once the record appears, life will change enormously for Scott, Clint, Dave, and Bob.

At least they'll be ready for it. The adulation they've received in Canada, Europe, and Asia has prepared them for America, and they've lived in the U.S. long enough to know what the country's like. They saw what happened with Hanson, so they know what's almost certainly in store for them. They're cute as can be, they're teens, they play their own instruments, sing beautifully, and even write some of their material. They're down-to-earth, polite, exactly the type of boy you could happily take home to mom without having to feel embarrassed. They're exactly what every girl wants waiting for her—someone lovely and talented. On top of that, they give encouragement to every teenage boy (and girl) playing in a band—it can happen to you, too.

"There's always kids in garage bands that love playing music but nobody's behind them to support them," Clint points out.

They've been lucky, it's true, but they've been lucky because they had talent, and they've been able to work well together—pretty amazing for a group of brothers, as anyone with a brother can tell you!

Although they've spent so much time together, far more than any family usually does, they still manage to get along well—no real fights, which is probably just as well, since they're all well trained in kung fu—Scott is a green belt, the others are all blue belts. And they have very different personalities.

"We're totally individual," Dave admits. "I'm the business-oriented one; quiet; shy; and I get embarrassed easily." Not so embarrassed that he's not the most competitive Moffatt, perhaps because he's the oldest of the triplets—Bob and Clint are identical twins, and just fractionally younger than him. In school the two of them thought alike, and even went for the same questions on tests. Their teachers used to think they were cribbing from each other, until they put them in separate rooms and found them still doing the same thing! Nowadays there are more differences between them. By his own admission, Dave is "very, very gabby," while Clint is the comedian of the band, with his jokes and love of practical jokes. Scott, that vital year older, is something of the leader, and much more intense in his attitude.

It's a family thing, and they say that the family that plays together, stays together. Well, the Moffatts have been playing together for ten years, since Dave first picked up the microphone his mom was going to use, and there have been no signs yet of those "artistic differences" that break up

THE MOFFATTS

bands. Much of the credit must go to their dad, Frank, who still coordinates everything for them, and makes sure nothing gets too far out of hand. Their stepmother, Sheila, who was a dental assistant, now handles all their makeup, while Darlana, their real mother, is fashioning a career for herself in Nashville as a singer—so the guys all get to see her, too, when they're home, and still keep in close contact with her.

Of course, by the time they *do* get home from their travels, there's not too much rest in store. When you're getting ten thousand pieces of fan mail a week, from all over the globe, that means you've got some serious work to do answering them all—especially if you've been gone a month or more, as the boys often are. That, however, is the price of fame, and it's one they're happy to pay.

For all that they've spent most of their lives in the spotlight, these are four boys who have managed to keep their feet very firmly planted on the ground. A lot of that is due to parental work, but also the fact that they've spent a lot of time working all over before becoming stars. It might seem like it to most people who don't know them, but their fame is far from sudden—there's a lot of groundwork, gigs, rehearsal, and recording before it all happened, which has given them a very good, and very realistic approach to what's happening now.

"Celebrities, to tell you the truth, are not important," is Scott's opinion. "So, when we walk on stage, it's not that we're celebrities. It's that we're making music that people can enjoy."

And that's the bottom line. They love rock, and they want to rock you. Sure, there are also some lovely ballads among the songs they've penned—and they've written more than a hundred so far—but it's the crunch of the guitars and the thump of the drums that makes them happy these days. And if it makes them happy, they hope it'll make *you* happy, too.

While they're doing this because music is what they

love, they're realistic enough to know that love alone doesn't pay the bills.

Scott said, "The only way for us to make money is to be known and have people talking about you and buying your albums. So, it's very important to have those people talking about you and, you know, having fans going crazy over you."

And they might as well get used to fans going crazy over them. It's happened everywhere else, and now it's happening in America, possibly on an even larger scale than anything they've ever experienced before. The time is right for them. They might have inspired Hanson, but it was Hanson who paved the way for them. People love boy bands, and well they should, but people like to rock, too, and the Moffatts deliver more than their share of that. Unlike Hanson, whose sound was based in old rock'n'roll, Scott, Clint, Bob, and Dave have listened to a lot of newer stuff. In them you can hear Nirvana (particularly in a song like "Wild at Heart") and Bush, among others. You won't find hip-hop or rap, just lots of real instruments played by real people. And there's absolutely nothing wrong with that. You can't be into everything, at least not if you're a musician. You have to make some choices about what to keep in and what to leave out. And the brothers know what they want to keep in. And so you won't find them boarding, for example. As they say, "Skating is more the hip-hop thing. We're more into rock."

One thing you shouldn't do is make the mistake of thinking of the Moffatts as just another Hanson. The only similarity is that both bands are made up of brothers, and they play their own instruments. But there are other rocks bands with brothers in them. How about Van Halen, with Eddie and Alex Van Halen? They've managed to carve out a pretty successful career for themselves. And so have Oasis, with Noel and Liam Gallagher, even if they do fight all the time. The point is, being brothers in a band doesn't automatically mean you're the same as any other band containing brothers. *Every* band works hard to develop its own sound, something that makes them individual, something that's recognizable, but still moves ahead from record to record. If there's a chemistry between the members, then the chances are they'll stay together. And maybe it *is* easier for brothers to develop a chemistry in their music, knowing each other so well. It certainly seems to have worked for the Moffatts. They've grown in the same direction at the same time. Where they'll end up is anyone's guess—even they don't really know—but along the way they'll make some great music and have plenty of fun. This is all they've ever wanted to do, and they're lucky to have achieved their dreams at such a young age.

Still, it's a long way from a town called Whitehorse, in the Yukon, or even from Victoria, British Columbia, to the big stages of the world, or even from the "Caterpillar Crawl" to "Until You Loved Me" or "If Life is So Short." It's been, literally, the trip of a lifetime. With all four brothers being so close in age, they've shared everything, all the growing up, all the experiences, and even the rough times that have happened. But that's what family is all about. They're always there to go through it with you, the good times and the bad. And without a doubt, the Moffatts are more than a band—they're family, too.

PART ONE
THE EARLY YEARS

CHAPTER 1

The town of Whitehorse, in Canada's Yukon Territory, isn't really near anywhere. If you look at a map, it sits above British Columbia, just next to Alaska, covering a vast amount of ground, stretching north past the Arctic Circle, all the way to the Beaufort Sea. Not exactly the warmest place in the world!

The closest city to Whitehorse is Juneau, Alaska, some two hundred and fifty miles *south*, two borders and another country away, and for much of the year, not an easy drive. For all its isolation, though, Whitehorse has some advantages. The air is clean, pristine. It's a place where people are used to being self-sufficient, in great part because they have to be, making their own entertainment, becoming friends. It had played an important part in the 1890s Gold Rush, back when paddle-wheel steamers went by the city on the Yukon River, and the air was full of the smell of sourdough bread—one of the food staples for the hopeful gold miners. Back then, with people panning for the yellow metal in the Klondike, it had been a major city.

All that was history, however, and now Whitehorse is another Canadian city. It hadn't stopped living in the 1890s, though—it is every bit as modern as anywhere else, with up-to-date businesses, malls, everything you'd find anywhere else. Maybe, because it remained on the frontier, it is a little less stuffy than most cities. And let's face it, it's hard to be stuffy when you spend most of the year bundled up to keep warm (the average springtime daily temperature is well below freezing).

Whitehorse was where Frank and Darlana Moffatt were living in 1983. There was a world of difference between Whitehorse and Vancouver, British Columbia, where they'd both grown up, met, and married. Vancouver could get chilly, but never the way the Yukon did. Being on the water meant that Vancouver generally enjoyed a fairly mild climate, even when the snow sometimes fell in winter. If you wanted to ski, there was always the resort of Whistler, not too far away. Vancouver was cosmopolitan, one of Canada's business centers, and its Pacific Rim city. It was constantly growing, the high-rise apartment buildings going up, houses stretching east and south from the city into communities like Surrey and Richmond.

But you went where the work was, and Whitehorse was where Frank was working. He was twenty-eight years old then. Since he was a teenager he'd sung, on and off, with bands. He loved music, and like so many of his generation, he'd essentially grown up with people like the Beatles and the Rolling Stones, listening to the radio and hearing the hits from Motown and all the other pop music of the time. It was in his blood.

Darlana, too, was a singer, but her leanings were more toward jazz. In fact, in 1978 she'd been named Top Canadian Jazz Vocalist, a great achievement for someone barely in her twenties. But jazz wasn't her only love; she'd developed a real affection for country music, too. That was back when country was still really country, before it exploded out of Nashville and all across America in the late Eighties, and all the baby boomers who'd become turned off by the way rock had changed all took to country. It was before the phenomenon known as Garth Brooks had made country massive, before Shania Twain (another Canadian) became only the third woman (after Whitney and Mariah) to have two albums go diamond—each sell more than ten million copies. So back then Darlana Moffatt was still in a minority, liking country before country was cool, as the song went.

Whitehorse wasn't the place where either of them would be by choice, but work was work, and Frank was making decent money there, which was just as well, because as 1983 began, Darlana was heavily pregnant with their first child, which meant another mouth to feed and even more expenses. It wasn't cheap to live in Whitehorse, since almost everything had to be brought in, but it was still cheaper than Vancouver, one of Canada's most expensive cities.

And it was in Whitehorse that Scott Andrew Moffatt was born, on March 30, 1983. He was everything Frank and Darlana had hoped he would be, a healthy baby boy who seemed to resemble both his father and his mother at the same time.

Becoming parents was a joy, but it also raised questions for Frank and Darlana. Whitehorse really wasn't the place where they wanted to stay and raise their son, plus the other children they hoped would follow in good time. A town where it was well below freezing for a good part of the year simply wasn't that child-friendly. They wanted Scott to be able to get outside and play, to be exposed to the kind of things they'd been exposed to. And that simply wasn't going to happen anywhere in the Yukon. Unless he was going to work in the oil business or start a whole new gold rush, there wasn't the kind of future here that they wanted for their son. That meant they'd have to move, and the obvious place was back to the West Coast, where they'd started.

After a lot of discussion, they decided that was the only course. But not to Vancouver, wonderful as the city was. They'd go a little further west, just off the coast, to Vancouver Island, and settle in the capital of British Columbia, Victoria. It was a little cheaper, there were jobs there, and it was still only a short ferry ride from the big city of Vancouver and their parents.

Apart from being the provincial capital, Victoria was

also a big tourist magnet. Ferries arrived from Vancouver and Seattle every day, and seaplanes landed in the harbor, all bringing tourists. The place was very English (it had a reputation at the time of being more English than England), well-kept, and looked a lot older than it was. The city's grand hotel, the Empress, kept up the grand British tradition of afternoon tea—sandwiches with the crusts removed, a selection of cakes, and tea—served every day at four P.M., something that attracted a lot of outsiders just for the novelty, especially since the British hadn't really indulged in proper afternoon tea for more than half a century. It was the *idea* that was important.

Apart from the Empress and the lovely, formal government buildings, Vancouver Island boasted one other big tourist attraction—Butchart Gardens, located a few miles out of town. Every spring and summer it became a massive display of flowers and plants that drew gardening fans from all over the world. So, all in all, it wasn't a bad place for the Moffatts to start a new life with their son. Actually, by the time they moved there, they knew it would soon be *children*, as they discovered Darlana was going to have another baby in March of 1984.

They knew there was another one on the way, and they were overjoyed by that—a brother or sister just a year younger than Scott would work out really well. But when Darlana went to see the doctor for an examination, she received the shock of her life. After examining her and taking an ultrasound, he told her that she wasn't going to be having just one baby, but three! The odds against anyone having triplets were so high that Frank and Darlana had never even considered it. Even the chances of having twins were only one in fifty-seven—still not exactly likely. So it was good news, since each of the fetuses seemed healthy, but still something to make them sit up and think. They'd been anticipating one more child, and now they were going to be faced with three! That meant a lot more diapers, a lot less sleep at night (and remember, Scott wouldn't even be a year old when the others were born), and a lot more

THE MOFFATTS

expense. But they'd been blessed, and the children were going to be theirs to love and care for.

By the time March 8, 1984, rolled around, the family was settled in Victoria. That was when Darlana's labor began, and Frank took her to the hospital, grandparents caring for young Scott. Giving birth to one had been difficult enough, but three at one time seemed more than three times the work. Bob proved to be the eldest by a few minutes, followed by his identical twin, Clint, and then finally Dave. Their full names were Clinton Thomas James Moffatt, Robert Franklin Peter Moffatt, and David Michael William Moffatt, and once they were strong enough they all came home with their mother. Not surprisingly, they'd all had slightly low birth weights, and the hospital wanted to keep them as patients for a few days to make sure everything was fine (and to give Darlana a chance to get her strength back before having to take of them, too). In fact, Clint stayed in the hospital longer than the others. He'd been born with a hernia, and needed an operation to correct that before he could come home. That was the first evidence of the special bond he and Bob share. The operation was done at night, finishing around four in the morning.

"We were in Victoria and Clint was in, I think, Vancouver. I woke up at four o'clock on the morning and started crying too," said Bob.

It wasn't easy, looking after four babies. As Frank described it, he and his wife quickly became "the fastest diaper changers in Canada," a talent they never knew they possessed. But in the next few years they'd all find themselves surprised by talents in the family.

Taking care of the kids was a full-time job in itself, but Darlana had never lost her singing ambitions. It wasn't that long since she'd been an up-and-coming performer, and she still had every desire to make it as a country singer. While doing it for a living seemed to be out of the question until the boys were a little older, there was nothing to stop her singing at charity shows and pageants around Victoria, which she was happy to do, while Frank looked after their sons. His own singing ambitions were behind him now, but he fully supported his wife, and took the kids to watch her when he could.

Getting by wasn't easy. They say two can live as cheaply as one, but six can only live as cheaply as six, at least when four of them are constantly growing, needing new clothes, and hungry and wanting to eat. Frank's energies were concentrated on simply supporting his family. He wanted his wife to succeed as a singer, since that was her dream, but his main priority in life had to be paying the bills and keeping a roof over their heads. So while Frank and Darlana might dream of a future for themselves, for the moment that was pretty much all it could be—a dream.

One thing they always did, however, was take the boys along when Darlana was rehearsing a performance. It would usually be in the daytime, on a weekend. So, even if they couldn't stay up for the actual show itself, they did at least get to hear their mother sing. By the time they were toddlers, the stage, concert hall, or even a gymnasium didn't seem such a strange place to them. They were, for the most part, well behaved—or as well-behaved as any group of boys can be. Scott, being a year older, was the undoubted leader, but already each of them had his own personality. By the time Scott was five and the others four, in the summer of 1988, they'd become a curious bunch, examining everything, wanting to expand the limits of their world, to push the envelope a little bit. That was perfectly natural, but it meant that their parents had to keep a close watch on them—not easy when you have four kids to keep an eye on!

As the boys had grown a little, it was easier for Darlana to return to singing. They still needed a lot of attention, but it wasn't as constant as when they'd been younger. She could find a little time for herself here and there, to rehearse, to sing. There was always music playing around the house, and the boys were used to having it in the background.

This one particular weekend Darlana had a gig, singing

at a teenage beauty pageant. It probably wasn't her first choice of venue—she'd rather have been singing in a recording studio, probably—but for the moment she was happy with what was available. She'd gone down before the show to rehearse with the band and do a sound check, to make sure the levels for instruments and voices were fine.

Frank had brought the boys along to watch her. The show itself would take place in the evening, long after their bedtime, and this way they could at least hear their mother sing. Since they'd become inquisitive, as all boys do, keeping them all together at one time was a difficult job. One would stray off for something, and by the time he'd been corralled, another one would disappear. So when Frank saw that Dave was missing, he knew he was close by somewhere, and began looking for him, telling the others to stay exactly where they were.

Dave had seen his mommy on the stage, singing, and he wanted to be close to her. So that was where he headed. It took a little time for him to find his way there, round the back stairs, but eventually he made it. That was where mom was and that was where he needed to be, by her. For the first couple of minutes, the music, and her voice, guided him. But that stopped. By the time he made his way onto the stage, Darlana had gone, leaving the microphone lying on the floor.

It was still on, since sound check hadn't ended yet. And since it was just there, it seemed the most natural thing in the world for Dave to pick it up. After all, his mother had been holding it. And then it seemed perfectly normal to start singing; that was what Darlana had been doing. Instead of a country song, however, Dave began to sing his favorite song, "Somewhere Out There," from *An American Tail*, the Steven Spielberg-produced animated feature that had been a big hit a couple of years before, and which he loved on video.

As he began to sing, all activity in the theater stopped. Suddenly Frank knew where his son was. Scott, Clint, and

Bob were amazed to see Dave up there, warbling away, since he was usually so shy. Darlana, who'd been taking a short break, recognized the voice, and turned to watch him. The crew, and the show's producers, all listened. Sure, it was cute to see a little boy up there singing, but more than that, Dave had a good voice. He was singing the song, he said later, "just like the mouse in the movie." He ran through the whole thing, and suddenly everyone was applauding him. Frank and Darlana were waiting in the wings to congratulate him, not even mad that he'd disappeared. In fact, they were proud of him, even if his brothers ended up teasing him (although they were actually a bit in awe) when he sat down with them.

Meanwhile, the show's producers were in a hurried conference with Frank and Darlana. Dave had been so impressive that they wanted to add him to the bill that night, singing the same song.

It was a big decision to make. Yes, he'd seemed like a natural up there, but how would he react when there was an audience staring up at him? And how would his brothers feel about him being singled out?

After sitting and talking to the boys, Frank and Darlana were a bit astonished. It turned out that Dave's brothers were actually a bit jealous of him being up there, and that he was eager to have the chance to show off in front of people! They knew the kids liked singing, but they'd never realized quite how much. So it was agreed that Dave would sing his solo that night, reprising his performance of "Somewhere Out There." As the time neared for her son to go onstage, however, Darlana, audience-seasoned, couldn't help but wonder if Dave would succumb to stage fright.

He didn't. Instead, he took to it like a duck to water, enjoying the feel, the spotlights on him—and most particularly the standing ovation he received when he finished. Dave Moffatt was the hit of the whole evening, a bigger success than his mom, who was overjoyed for him. Right then and there, Dave knew what he wanted to do. And

THE MOFFATTS

when he told his brothers, they agreed it was what they wanted to do, too.

One show doesn't make a career, though. He'd been applauded as much for being cute as being good. A four-year-old singing on stage is a novelty, and the Moffatts didn't want their kids to be thought of that way. If they were going to sing, it would be because they wanted to, and because they were good. A couple of weeks passed, and the boys began to forget all about Dave and the teen pageant. Summer was here and there was too much to do, time to spend outdoors, games to be played. Frank and Darlana were glad that the idea faded. The boys needed a real childhood, to grow up at their own pace. They knew all too well how fragile show business could be, how it was full of disappointments—exactly what they didn't want for their family.

Later in the summer they decided to take a trip a bit east from Victoria, to the interior of western Canada, and most specifically to Edmonton in Alberta, some five hundred miles from home. The boys were old enough for a fairly short road trip. It would be a change of scene, and give them all a chance to see some of the country. It was rugged and barren in the mountains, but still majestic, the views going on for miles, the skies clear and blue. They all sang along to the radio and to tapes as they drove, throughly enjoying a real family vacation.

One place they just had to visit on their trip was West Edmonton Mall. It was by far the largest mall in Canada, and at the time quite possibly the largest in North America. It advertised regularly on CBC, the Canadian broadcasting network. It was so big, in fact, that some people even took their vacations there! Hotels had sprung up around it, making it one of the ultimate shopping experiences.

The Moffatts were familiar with the malls around Vancouver, but this was way bigger, the kind of place where you could easily spend several hours just window-shopping. And that was all they intended to do—they hadn't traveled so far just to go shopping—until they saw one particular store. There you could make a record of yourself singing, a little souvenir of your visit. Right then and there they all decided to do it, something for the boys' grandparents to play. Given who it was for, the choice of song was immediately obvious. "Grandpa (Tell Me 'Bout The Good Ole Days)" had been a hit for the Judds, Naomi and her daughter, Wynonna. The family knew it—they'd sung it in the car as they traveled. The boys would sing the verses, and then Frank and Darlana would add their voices on the chorus. It seemed simple enough. They paid their money, packed the six of them into the booth, and waited for the red light to come on, signaling that the recording had begun.

What they didn't realize was that the store's owner could pipe the singing into the mall, and as soon as he heard the boys' sweet voices in a natural harmony, that was exactly what he did. Unaware of what was happening, the family sang on, making it all the way through. Meanwhile, outside, people were stopping to listen. One or two at first, then more, and more, until, by the time they were finished, there was a whole crowd outside the store, hanging on to the sound. As Frank, Darlana, and the boys emerged from the booth to wait for their record, they were greeted by applause from the crowd, which was more than a small shock at the time. Once the store's owner explained what he'd done, and played the disc back for them, they realized that the boys really had something. They sounded *great*, and they began to realize why everyone had stopped to listen. More to the point, the kids thought it was a blast.

That the boys had talent was beyond question. This went way past cute. Brothers have always had a natural harmony with each other (going back to the Fifties, the Everly Brothers were a prime example), something that just couldn't be copied, and Scott, Dave, Clint, and Bob definitely had it. But there was even more. They projected, they sounded older than their years, as if they really got into the song. The question was what they should do with all this. . . .

Well, the first thing, once they arrived home, was to give

the discs they'd made to their grandparents. That was why they'd made them in the first place. But the boys were eager to do more singing in front of people. Frank made a few phone calls, and soon managed to land them on a charity show in Victoria.

Now that they had a gig, the next thing they needed was an act, and that meant some songs. The obvious direction for them to go was country, not just because it was the music they heard at home all the time, but also, as Bob notes, "Country music was like it could suit our age because we were singing about 'I think she likes me' and stuff. But to go on stage and do the rock deal was not suitable for our age."

It helped that they already knew some country songs, from singing them around the house and in the car, so figuring out which ones to do wasn't all that difficult. They had some simple costumes, and a few basic moves, but the idea was that they'd get by, for as long as their interest lasted, mostly on their singing talent.

The truth was, neither Frank nor Darlana thought this would last. They were kids, after all, whose interests and ambitions changed from day to day. By the time they'd played a couple of shows, they'd probably be bored with it and ready to move on to something else. That was fine with their parents; it was part of the process of growing up. For now they could indulge the kids a little, and see how they fared.

The answer was, much better than anyone had imagined. The audiences loved them—it was difficult to resist four smiles, the cute faces, and the very professional-sounding voices covering the country hits. One show led to another, and another, more by word of mouth than anything. They were all charity events, with the Moffatt Brothers, as they were billed, not being paid for their appearances.

By the time Christmas rolled around, they had a few shows under their belt, and their interest showed absolutely no sing of flagging—quite the opposite. They loved being up there, entertaining people, and, above all, singing together. It was as if they'd been born to do exactly this. Their parents were surprised, but happy. Loving music themselves, they were glad to see the kids enjoying it, even if it was in a way they hadn't anticipated. Already Frank was getting phone calls about booking them for charity and community shows the following summer, not just in Victoria, but all over British Columbia. The word was spreading much more quickly than he could have imagined. The Moffatt Brothers were getting popular!

Their fame was spreading, and it even reached the ears of Victoria radio station CFAX. To them, it seemed like a natural idea to sponsor the group in their local appearances, and that was exactly what they did, sending them out in CFAX T-shirts, and arranging a backdrop for the stages that advertised both band and station. At one event they even got to meet the Canadian Prime Minister, Brian Mulroney, who was from the province.

The Moffatt Brothers received a big boost when they were asked to perform on the Easter Seals telethon, singing live on the British Columbia segment. Suddenly they went from being a small-time attraction to something much bigger, reaching a wider audience than any personal appearance could manage. They were a big hit there, and that, inevitably, led to more bookings.

Even now, Frank wasn't thinking of money for the boys. As long as their expenses were covered, everything was fine. It still seemed as if it might be a phase, even though they were heading off every weekend to play somewhere in B.C. Doing it for charity was a way of giving something back, of being grateful for all the things they *did* have. And this way it didn't become a career, thinking of how much they could make. It was better to keep it simple like this. That way they could stop any time they wanted—and he felt sure that sooner, rather than later, they'd be ready to move on to something else.

CHAPTER 2

But as another summer passed, that really didn't seem to be the case. The boys loved what they were doing and looked forward to the weekends, the traveling and singing, more than anything else. They'd worked up more songs and had a real act going now. They still traded a lot on their cuteness, but the more they sang, the more it became apparent that those voices were really something. People were reacting more to the singing than the way they looked these days, and the more they played and rehearsed, the more professional they sounded. They were earning a reputation, and it was more than justified.

Winter was a hard time for the boys. After thoroughly enjoying themselves all summer playing shows, it seemed like there was nothing to do. But in 1989, once summer had passed, there was a change—Scott started school. The triplets were still at home, and suddenly everything seemed different. Instead of being all together, all the time, it was as if someone broke them up every day. But that was the way of things. He had to go to school. Another year and they'd be joining him, which wouldn't be too bad. For now, though, it just didn't feel right to any of them. The fact that, for the most part, their weekends were empty only made it worse. They'd acquired a real taste for music and for singing, and now there was nowhere to indulge that—not until the weather grew warmer and the sun came out again. Winters in the Pacific Northwest are often long and gray, with a depressing light rain falling almost every day. This particular winter seemed longer than all the ones that had gone before.

Frank and Darlana (who was still working on her own singing career) looked forward to more charity work with the boys in 1990. For now, with them still so young, it seemed like the right thing to do. They didn't know that the Moffatt Brothers had been spotted by bookers for some of the Canadian country music festivals.

Country had come a long way in the last couple of years, even north of the border. Musically, it was now a very big deal. A lot of baby boomers had begun buying country albums, and the sound became more accessible, moving away from the "hillbilly" image that had kept it from a massive mainstream audience for years. Artists like Foster and Lloyd, out of Nashville, could sound both country and poppy. If it still hadn't become as big as it would in a few years, things were moving. Probably Canada's premier country singer was Michelle Wright, who, apart from having her own records, also hosted a regular country show on CBC, making her into a national name and a proven attraction. But other acts, like Blue Rodeo, were also quite big—even if they meant next to nothing in the U.S.

The country music festivals in Canada drew a lot of people, even if many of the acts had to be imported from the south. As of yet, there was no Shania Twain, no Canadian country megastar—it was a field that was still very young there. And the very young Moffatt Brothers fit in perfectly.

For the boys, this was the big time. They'd be traveling all over the country, and Canada is one of the biggest countries in the world. Best of all, they'd get to sing to big crowds of people. To help keep their feet firmly on the ground, Frank arranged the festival dates in between local charity events. He didn't want them getting big heads, thinking and acting like they were stars. He wanted them completely aware of who they were, where they were from,

THE MOFFATTS

and the debt they owed people locally who'd first supported them.

Being backstage at the festivals was unlike anything the brothers had experienced. Everywhere they looked there were singers and musicians, people playing guitars. The crowds were bigger than any they'd ever sung for, and they were all there to have a good time and hear some great music. They got to be fans themselves, meeting artists they'd only heard on record; it was a very big deal. And it wasn't just happening once. There were a number of these events over the course of the summer, taking them from Ontario and Quebec all the way back west to British Columbia. It was like being paid to do what they loved and have a cool geography lesson thrown in, too. They loved every minute of it. More importantly, the crowds loved *them*.

The Moffatt Brothers were now officially professionals, having been paid for their appearances. That didn't make them stars, but it was the first real step on the journey they've been undertaking ever since. The impression they made on people lasted long after they'd left the stage. People wanted more of them.

And they wanted more of the people. It seemed like this definitely wasn't a phase for the boys, after all. They loved every minute of it, as if this was the thing they'd been born to do and they'd discovered it early. Traveling had been great fun, seeing new places, meeting new people, and they were ready for more of it—lots more. As fall came, and their performing season ended, with all of them now in school, they pestered their parents for more shows. It was what they wanted to do.

It wasn't as if the offers weren't coming in. Since the festivals, Frank's phone had been ringing regularly with offers of gigs all across the country. People genuinely liked what Scott, Clint, Bob, and Dave were doing, and for a lot more than the novelty factor. Others were realizing what their parents and those around Victoria had known for a couple of years—they were good, natural talents.

So far, though, they'd had it easy. They'd been flown in for the festivals, and then it was back home again. And in B.C. there'd been friends to stay with, or they'd performed close enough to home to be in their own beds at night. Frank knew well enough that real touring was a lot harder than that. It meant long drives every day, not enough sleep, and having to give your all to a crowd every night, even when you didn't feel up to it. He explained that to his sons, but they weren't about to be discouraged. The little taste of performing that they'd had simply whetted their appetite.

Thinking about it and actually doing it were two different things, Frank knew all too well, but as they continued asking him to set up shows, he went ahead and booked a tour for the summer of 1991. There would be a total of forty dates, taking them all the way across the country, and it would be a massive family road trip. But, he told the boys, they'd committed themselves now. They had a responsibility. If they got tired of it halfway through, they still had to go on, because they'd promised. Did they understand that?

They understood it, and they were happy about it. For the boys, summer and the end of school couldn't come soon enough. They were ready to get in the car and take off *now*.

In fact, they didn't know how lucky they were. To be able to book a national, forty-date tour for any act was pretty remarkable. To do it for one that was largely unknown, and who didn't have a record out, was little short of miraculous. But the Moffatt Brothers obviously had gathered fans all over.

It was with a huge sense of anticipation that the family loaded up the car just after school let out for the year. The weather was good, and the next two and a half months were going to be filled with singing and fun and travel—it was everything the boys could have hoped for.

Of course, they weren't going to be playing the kind of venues they do these days when they hit the road. No arenas. They couldn't even play clubs, since they were way under age to be allowed in there, even as performers. And, because they weren't well known, and had no record out, the best they could hope for was a series of small shows, taking in enough money to cover their expenses, so no one lost any money from all this time on tour—both Frank and Darlana had taken leaves from their regular jobs.

Secretly, Frank was hoping that the boys would get heartily sick of touring after twenty or so dates. The repetition—travel, motel, gig, motel, travel—could easily get to them. It might have sounded glamorous, but the reality of life in a band moving around was really boring, and young kids get bored very easily. He wanted to discourage them, or at least make them very aware of the harsh realities of life in the music business. It would be for their own good, really. Not that he wanted to turn them away from music, which they obviously loved. But there was plenty of time ahead for that. For now, there was a childhood to be enjoyed, friends to play with, imaginations to be loosed, all of which was very different from a family packed into a car with their luggage, making their way slowly east, day by day, show by show.

Canada is a huge country. While Highway 401 goes across it, the Moffatts didn't spend much time on that. Instead they were going from town to town, some big, most small, on big highways and two-lane roads, singing for their supper, gas money, a bed for the night, and a little more. To the kids, it was one giant adventure. There was always something new to see, traveling the prairies of Alberta and Saskatchewan, going over the Rockies, heading into the heavily populated areas of Ontario, then the French-speaking province of Quebec, still part of the same country, but somehow so different, then on to the Eastern seaboard areas of Nova Scotia and Newfoundland, before turning around and slowly heading back home. There was no doubt they'd seen the country in a way few kids their age could have, not just watching it from a window, but having contact every day with people, entertaining them, making new friends all over.

Frank found, to his surprise, that his plan had completely

backfired. The boys loved the traveling, and, most of all, the performing to people every day. It was in their blood, inherited from their parents, and it simply wasn't going to be denied. It didn't matter whether they drew five people or five hundred, they just loved what they were doing, and it showed. Their enthusiasm was infectious, and the audiences went away having had a good time, completely entertained by the boys, who were then just eight and seven, but already veteran performers—and becoming better singers every year.

So, instead of being bored with touring, by the time they drove back into Victoria, Scott, Clint, Dave, and Bob were quite ready to turn around and do it all over again. Which was more than Frank and Darlana were: It had been a long summer for them, with driving, organizing everything, and trying to make sure it all went off as smoothly as possible. They were ready for school to begin, and to have a little rest.

It had all gone well, but the parents still weren't really thinking of this in terms of a career for the boys. Let them grow up a little and have some fun and freedom first. They didn't want to be showbiz parents, pushing their boys to succeed and do more and more. The world would do that to them soon enough, anyway. For the summer performing was fine. But Frank and Darlana weren't even hungry to find a record deal for the kids, although they'd have almost certainly been able to if they'd wanted. But that would have taken it to another level, one they weren't ready to reach for yet. It would all have become *too* serious then.

As always, to the boys winter seemed to last forever, damp and gloomy, with nothing to occupy their weekends, no trips, no singing, and above all, no performing. Sure, they liked soccer and hockey and football, all the normal physical activities boys got up to, but what they really loved to do was sing. Unusually for brothers, they liked being together. Dave and Bob actually sat next to each other in school.

"[T]hey thought we were cheating because we always

chose the same questions," remembers Dave. "So they put us in different rooms and still we would have the same questions and the same right or wrong answers as we write our answers the same way."

Then again, it probably wasn't *too* surprising, given that they really were identical twins. Not only did they look alike, they thought completely alike, too. And just like their other two brothers, they were crazy about music.

Winter was turning to spring in 1992 when they got a huge surprise and boost. They hadn't been expecting it, since they weren't adult performers, but the Moffatt Brothers found themselves nominated for five awards from the British Columbia Country Music Association. Now that was a very big deal. They'd been playing around the province for a couple of years, and they were one of the few local acts who'd managed to tour nationally, but it wasn't as if they had an album or even a single.

But the fact was that they were good, and a lot of people recognized that, and were willing to give them credit for it. All too often people say that it's enough of a honor just to be nominated for an award. For the brothers, that was definitely true, and to be nominated in five categories was amazing. Of course, they, along with their parents, had to attend the awards ceremony. It was the polite thing to do, even if most of it took place after their bedtime. On some occasions you could make an exception.

In the end, they didn't walk away with any of the awards, but that really didn't matter. They'd been acknowledged by people who knew country music, and accepted as strong local performers. For now, that was ample. They had many years ahead to collect awards and trophies.

The country music labels in Nashville were always on the lookout for fresh talent, and it wasn't unusual to see producers and talent scouts from Music City in all different parts of North America, looking eagerly for the next big act. In fact, one of them had flown up for the awards ceremony in Vancouver. His name was Robert Byrne, a producer who'd enjoyed some success, and was looking for a band that was fresh and had something new to offer. He talked to Frank and Darlana, and took a tape of the boys home with him.

In 1992, Nashville still hadn't discovered teen artists. The phenomenon known as LeAnn Rimes was still four years away from happening (she's actually just seven months older than Scott Moffatt). Garth Brooks had hit big, and in his wake were coming a whole slew of identical "hat acts"—guys wearing Stetsons, singing in deep voices. It was a lot of things, but how country it was remained to be decided. What no one could deny was that it was successful.

When Byrne listened to the tape of the brothers, he was far more impressed than he'd expected. Before hearing them, he figured that they'd been nominated because they were cute and something of a novelty. While that might have been partly true at the beginning, by now they'd really developed into something special, something that, he thought, could have wider appeal to country fans. If anything, he was amazed that no one had snatched them up before, and that they didn't already have a recording contract. He gave Frank a call, and suggested that the family fly down to Nashville to cut a few tracks with him producing, and see what might come out of it.

While Frank had been hesitant before, wanting to protect his boys from the rough realities of the business side of music, he understood that this was an offer he couldn't turn down. The kids would be excited, there was no doubt about that, and it was the kind of break that might only come once. He had to take advantage of it, if only so they could see the inside of a recording studio and see what happened there, and hear what they really sounded like. The arrangements were made, and as soon as school let out, the family was driving to Vancouver International Airport, tickets in hand, to go to Nashville.

For Scott, Clint, Dave, and Bob, it all seemed like fun. Last summer Canada, this summer America. They could see the sights, maybe even meet some of their heros, and they'd be *recording*; this was the coolest thing that had happened yet. And even though being in the studio meant an awful lot of work, laying down lead vocals and harmonies, they loved every single second they were there. It was all magic to them. Five songs had been selected, the kind of things that didn't sound too strange for kids to be singing, and they worked hard, rehearsing, then doing take after take, going into the control room to hear them played back, while Byrne made suggestions to each of them to improve the performance.

This was what it was all about, hearing themselves properly, getting a real lesson in how to improve everything. Even though there was no guarantee of a record contract at the end of it, somehow that didn't matter. Just being here was enough for the moment, taking it all in, constantly learning.

When everything was complete, Frank, Darlana, and the boys headed home, where they had gigs scheduled for the rest of the long summer break, and Byrne sent his tape to all the contacts he had in Nashville. He believed in the Moffatt Brothers. He heard something in them that was quite special, even if they were still very young. They didn't just have potential—they were already achieving something.

He might have seen it, but it seemed as if no one else at the country labels did. Everyone turned him down. They were too young, too much of a novelty. They weren't what the labels were looking for at the moment. The focus was on men who could follow up on the fences Garth Brooks had broken down—his most recent album, *Ropin' The Wind*, had been the first country album to debut at the top of the *Billboard* pop charts, and would go on to sell ten million copies, as well as giving rise to three Number One singles—and everyone wanted something like that, not a bunch of kids.

That left one option—releasing it themselves. It was an expensive proposition, a gamble, but one that would prove worthwhile. For a while now, people had been wanting to buy a Moffatts record after seeing them live, and this would make the perfect souvenir. *Wonderful World*, as the record would be called, was taken from the tracks the brothers recorded in Nashville, as well as songs they completed in British Columbia.

A look at the track listing on the record, and some of the song titles, says a great deal about the kind of material the guys were singing back then: "What a Wonderful World," "Grandma," "We're Off to the Rodeo," "All I Have is a Dream," "Itty Bitty Smile," "Bird Dog," "I Think I'm Falling in Love," "Dogs is Dogs," "Do Wah Diddy Diddy," "That's All Right."

These would be the songs they'd be featuring on stage for the next several months as they went out to plug the record, at every show they'd end up playing. Sure, a lot of them fell into the "cute" category, but the brothers also managed to work their own special vocal magic on them.

When the album appeared, Scott and the triplets were eager to hold it in their hands, to have their work in front of them, something they'd done that they could show everyone. The cover was a black and white picture of them over a white background covered with random squiggles. It was something that just screamed "Buy Me!"

The well-known covers—tunes like "What a Wonderful World," which was written by the late singer Louis Armstrong, and had been a hit for a number of artists, the classic Manfred Mann Sixties hit "Do Wah Diddy Diddy," and the Everly Brothers "Bird Dog" (a song that might have been tailored for the Moffatts) all worked well enough, as did "That's All Right," the Arthur Crudup blues that Elvis had redone as one of the first real rock 'n' roll songs in 1954. Much of the rest of the material came from the pens of the family, part of their ever-increasing catalogue of songs.

In truth, it was a very strong collection for a bunch of kids, especially considering they'd helped write a lot of the songs. Yes, a lot of it had a very high cutesy quotient, but what could you expect when Scott wasn't even ten yet?

THE MOFFATTS

They were still young boys, and thinking in young boy ways. And the record proved beyond a shadow of a doubt that they could all sing like angels.

And putting out the record proved to be a great decision when a copy of it found its way into the hands of another singing family—the Osmonds.

CHAPTER 3

In their day—specifically between 1971 and 1978—the Osmonds had notched up an incredible twenty-three gold records, either together, or by Donny and Marrie Osmond as a duo or performing solo. They were one of the biggest pop acts to come out of America. There was Alan, Wayne, Merrill, Jay, Donny, Marie, and Jimmy. They were born and raised in Utah, all strict Mormons, which meant no smoking, drinking, not even any caffeine. But they could make music, and they grew up singing. In 1962 the four eldest boys went to Disneyland wearing matching suits, and were invited to perform by the house barbershop quartet (barbershop was a vintage singing style). After that they appeared on the television show hosted by crooner Andy Williams. And once they began recording, they seemed unstoppable. They were, in a way, the Moffatt Brothers of their day, although their music was very mainstream pop. The one who went country was Marie Osmond, who covered "Paper Roses" in 1973 and had a big hit with it. Donny and Marie had their own TV show. But, like everything else, time passed the Osmonds by. Marie kept a recording company, and Donny released records that didn't sell well, and ended up working in stage musicals.

But Branson, Missouri, was a place that welcomed the Osmonds. A lot of the older country acts who played in the style that was no longer fashionable in Nashville, had established theaters there, and it had become a resort that drew thousands of people every year, and still does. Maybe it wasn't hip, but it gave the people exactly what they wanted, and they kept coming back So even though the Osmonds had never been a country act before, there was nothing to stop them reinventing themselves as one (not unlike the way the Moffatts would reinvent themselves as a pop act, really), and set up their own theater there. The people who came to Branson would come into their theater, too. There'd never been anything extreme about the Osmonds; they'd always been so middle of the road they could have been the center stripes. And they could all play their own instruments.

Maybe they saw something of their younger selves in the brothers from Canada. Or maybe they just realized that the Moffatt Brothers were good. Whatever it was, they were impressed by the music that had been recorded in Nashville with Robert Byrne, impressed enough to contact Frank and offer the boys a chance to work at the Osmonds Theater in Branson.

It was the perfect place to start. The folks who visited didn't care if the acts had a new record out or not. They wanted to be entertained for a while, to hear something that wasn't a hat act or some girl who couldn't decide if she was country or pop. And the Moffatt Brothers were country.

It was a big offer, and it called for a big decision. This wasn't a deal for a single appearance, it was for a whole season, performing every day. That would mean a lot of changes. The whole family would have to move to Branson, a place very, very different from Victoria. It would, obviously, mean leaving Canada, the grandparents, aunts, uncles, and friends. And it would mean leaving school. If that were to happen, then the best option for Frank and Darlana would be to home school their sons. It was something they *could* do, but it would be a lot more work for them. Still, it would mean that the boys could have a full-time musical career, and that was essentially what the offer from the Osmonds meant—Scott, Clint, Dave, and Bob would be turning into professional singers at the age of nine and eight, respectively. It was young for that, in many ways, but how often would opportunities like this come around?

The only fair way was to discuss it with the kids, since it affected them more than anyone else. But it was no real surprise to hear that they were all in favor of the change, given the way they'd taken to touring. Frank tried to explain that this would be like being on the road. They'd be living in a small town, and there probably wouldn't even be many kids their own age around, but nothing was going to discourage them. They didn't know the Osmonds or their music, but that didn't matter. If they wanted them, then the Moffatt Brothers would be happy to go.

This was really different from leaving on tour. Everything was packed, some of the stuff in storage, the rest in a trailer behind the car, the necessities they couldn't live without. They'd be gone a few months, maybe forever—who knew? The ferry took them across to Vancouver, where the boys saw their grandparents, then it was south to the border, on to Interstate 5, and the big journey had begun.

More even than crossing Canada, the journey took them through different cultures. There was the Northwest, so familiar to them, then the West of the cowboys, with towns few and far between, the Teton Mountains in Wyoming dwarfing the ranches below, the beauty and green of Colorado, the flatness of Kansas, which really did seem to have amber waves of grain growing as far as the eye could see. It was only late spring, but as they reached the center of America, it was hot, and even more humid. Growing up on the West Coast, the kids had never really encountered humidity before. And it would only get worse as summer progressed. It was a relief to reach the motel every night and turn on the air conditioning. As Frank pointed out to them, though, they might as well get used to it quickly.

They were going to be living with the humidity for a long time.

Branson seemed more like a place given over to a theme park than a town. Many artists had their theaters here, and they'd appear themselves regularly. There were souvenir shops and restaurants, along with any number of motels and RV parks, which always seemed to be full of tourists. And the tourists always seemed to be older, often retired, spending some time in Branson, located in the Ozark mountains. It was a place for them to relive memories of singers they'd enjoyed long ago, before country changed and became big musical business.

But the Osmond family couldn't have been nicer to the Moffatts. Having gone through show business themselves, they knew full well what it was like for kids, what the pressures could be—and how to avoid them. They'd be performing regularly, but it wasn't the most punishing schedule, not even as demanding as the tour across Canada that they'd done. There would be plenty of time for school every day with Frank and Darlana, and time to just play, and really be kids, as well as rehearse and do their shows. As an introduction to the professional life, it was probably perfect.

Getting back to a regular schedule of gigs was good for the boys. They had an act rehearsed, songs they and their parents loved, a lot of it older country that would be more familiar to the Branson audience, but also some songs they'd written with Frank and Darlana that seemed to fit in well. And they had enough material to change things around a little, if something didn't seem to be working, or just for sheer variety.

It was a routine to get used to, appearing at the theater, having school with their parents, constantly learning. If the boys had hoped Frank and Darlana would go easy on them with lessons, they were sadly mistaken. Home schooling was a new thing to all of them, and the parents pushed the kids to make sure they'd be keeping up, maybe even more than if they'd been in regular school.

A lot of people saw the Moffatt Brothers perform in Branson, and they had the chance to see a lot of other people perform. It was a family-friendly place where entertainment was the key. Having so many veteran musicians and singers close by meant that they couldn't help but pick up some new ideas and learn a great deal to make them better at what they were doing. And something that would really help them improve would be learning to play instruments. In the theater they used a backing band, but if they could play the songs themselves, they could be completely self-contained.

For country music, guitar was the obvious choice, and Scott, the eldest, gravitated to that. He had first pick, and it wasn't long before he could hammer out a few chords. Clint took up the bass—not an easy instrument when your fingers are small. Bob found a set of drums, and Dave bought a keyboard. With no shortage of people around to give them lessons and pointers, they all developed quickly. Not to the point where they were ready to go and play in public (the people backing them were serious professional musicians), but enough to help them in writing songs. Having made the commitment to playing instruments, Frank and Darlana made sure they took time each day to practice. It was the only way to get better, to get their fingers supple, to learn all they needed to know. While the guys backing them made it all look incredibly easy, that was because they'd all put in many years learning their skill—and they had a lot of talent to begin with. The boys could sing, but did they have the talent to be instrumentalists?

It seemed as if they did. They picked things up quickly, and, most importantly, they could translate the sounds they heard in their heads into music with their fingers. They still weren't that great, finding their way around, but it was slowly getting there.

Playing was another string to their bow, although it was really something for the future more than the present. For right now they had to concentrate on the daily show, which was going over incredibly well. They made a lot of new fans and friends in Branson. They were still young enough to be considered really cute, and good enough to constantly surprise the people who came to hear them.

Among the crowds were always talent scouts, looking for up-and-coming acts for different shows. One of them proved to be from Las Vegas, of all places, and the show the Moffatt Brothers put on impressed him. Even if they didn't have a recording contract, they could still entertain, and they were slowly developing a reputation. After seeing them, he talked to Frank and Darlana.

Really, he couldn't have come along at a better time. The contract with the Osmond Theater was ending soon, and while it could have been renewed, the boys needed a new challenge. Branson was fun, but it was a little limiting. The boys were growing, eager to take on more and more. But Vegas was something totally unexpected. It had always seemed like the place for big-name entertainers to make big money. But there was more to it than that. The big names worked in the big rooms, and all the hotels and casinos had more than that. There were lounges and other entertainment rooms. The talent scout wondered if the Moffatts might be interested in taking their show to the Aladdin Hotel. Obviously, they wouldn't be headlining, but they'd be playing every day. It would be like Branson, but for more people—and for more money.

It was time for another big decision. The Osmonds had given them a break, and Branson had been good to them Las Vegas had a reputation for its gambling and nightlife. Was that the kind of place Frank and Darlana wanted to take their sons?

The thing to be remembered was that they were professionals now, and that meant weighing the available offers, and taking the best one. While Frank and Darlana wanted it to be fun for the boys, it was now their source of income—it was the income for the whole family, in fact, since the parents had left their jobs and their native country to look after their sons. And that meant taking the offer from Vegas. Initially it wasn't that long a contract, but if they did well, it would be renewed—and might be renewed several times. Scott was ten now, and the triplets nine. Frank and Darlana knew they'd brought them up right, and instilled good values in them, enough so that all the neon and gilt of The Strip wouldn't turn their heads away from who they were and what they wanted to do.

Las Vegas might only be two hundred and fifty miles from Los Angeles, the center of the music and film businesses in America, but that's a long way, and a lot of desert. In fact, Las Vegas sits like some surreal oasis in the middle of the desert, a city where none should be, by rights. Its water is all piped in to satisfy the needs of residents and visitors. Outside there's dry heat, and outside town the wilderness reclaims everything, but the streets of town seem to remain active twenty-four hours a day, the casinos and hotels some bizarre dream of past, present, and future all melded together and dropped in one unlikely place.

The first thing the family noticed was the climate. In Branson the humidity and heat had constantly sucked the energy from them. In the desert of the Southwest it was hotter, but drier; no humidity to speak of at all. Weatherwise, it was about as far away from the soggy Northwest as they could get and still be on the same continent.

Then they hit town, and everyone was staring, openmouthed, out of the windows. Frank and Darlana knew about Vegas, but the reality outstripped anything they'd heard or seen before. It was on a massive scale, the hotels, the casinos with their different motifs and styles, most of them a million miles from everyday America. It was life on a ridiculously grand scale. It was, deliberately, the kind of place meant to make people part with their money, a showbiz town, once a home away from home for singers like Frank Sinatra, Elvis, and Tom Jones. The biggest names in entertainment had played here at one time or another, and now the Moffatt Brothers would be joining the list.

One advantage of playing at a hotel was that there was no need to look for an apartment; there were rooms for the whole family. And even if it seemed odd to be setting up home in a hotel, there was still a sense of adventure about it, of doing something very different and very fun.

It was all quite strange at first, but very quickly the novelty wore off, and it was just like Branson, but in a different setting. Every morning there was school with Frank and Darlana, followed by rehearsal and time for the boys to practice their instruments. Living in the heart of the city, there wasn't too much chance to simply get out and play around, to kick a ball, throw a football. Most of the time, though, they could at least go swimming in the hotel pool.

There were a few days of rehearsal with the hotel band to get everything down in their act, and they had to adapt to a different stage with different dimensions. Once that was done, it was smooth sailing, and the boys settled into the routine of performing. The crowd was very different from what they'd known in Missouri or Canada, much less family-oriented. But they were still appreciative, and saw that the kids really did know what they were doing, that they'd become very seasoned professionals, and applauded them for it.

The first couple of weeks were really a case of settling in and getting used to the different circumstances. The rhythm of Vegas was completely different, faster, non-stop, and they had to adapt to that, both in their lives and their music. It wasn't a city designed for kids, and so the family had to find outlets, getting out of town, into the desert, where they could be away from everything.

But the money was good, they were drawing strong crowds, just by word of mouth. The staff at the Aladdin Hotel were extremely accommodating, wanting to make their stay as pleasant and home-like as possible. They hadn't been playing there long before their contract was extended, as sure a sign of success as they were likely to find. Even the high-rollers, the big gamblers that Vegas loved, enjoyed them, as well as the couples on charter trips for a few days. They were a hit right across the board with their sweet harmonies that touched the heart, mixing the upbeat songs with the tearjerkers, playing tunes that were familiar to the generally older crowd who came to see them.

By now, between Branson and Vegas, their reputation was beginning to spread, and a few Nashville executives were probably wishing they'd taken the plunge and signed the Moffatt Brothers when they'd had the chance. Frank was regularly receiving calls from labels, interested in the boys. For now, however, they were committed to Vegas, and there didn't seem to be any point in doing anything more until their contract expired. Since the hotel loved them, and kept renewing, increasing the money, that didn't look like it was happening any time soon.

But there was another side to the coin—how long did the family want to stay in Vegas? Recording was the way ahead, and hotel living was fine in the short-term, but they needed a home, with a yard, with some real freedom. The current contract extension meant they'd have been in Vegas seven months by the time it was over, and Frank, Darlana, and the boys decided that was enough. It had been a great experience, they'd loved it, but it was time to move on and try to break into the record business. After all, the interest was already there.

CHAPTER 4

So, in 1994, once again they packed up the car and the trailer and moved on. It was beginning to seem as if traveling was a constant in their lives since leaving Canada, with no chance to put down roots and make any close, lasting friends. Scott, Clint, Dave, and Bob missed their grandparents, and their old home, but they were thrilled at the prospect of possibly making a real record—assuming everything worked out. And now they were going to find out if it would. This was make-or-break time. They were headed back to Nashville.

Rolling into town again, the boys saw it in a completely different light. It was 1994, and two years had passed since they'd been here. In the meantime they'd done a lot of growing, not just physically, but as artists. They were confident in their abilities now, and they'd even improved by leaps and bounds as instrumentalists. The songs they were writing—along with Frank and Darlana, they'd composed thirty-five songs so far—were much better, true professional work. They felt they could hold their own against almost anyone.

Meetings had been set up with the interested labels, and offers were made. But Frank had left what he thought might be the best meeting until last. Robert Byrne, the man who'd first brought them to Nashville, and who'd had faith in them long before any of the other record companies, had taken a job with a label. He now held the title of vice president with Polydor Nashville—in other words, he'd become a major executive, with the power to sign whoever he wanted.

A couple of years before, the Moffatts had developed a good relationship with him, and appreciated all he'd done to help them. It was probably fair to say that without him they'd have still been in Canada, working fairs and charity shows, making forays across the country in summer—but the boys wouldn't be professional singers.

He was interested in having the Moffatt Brothers as Polydor recording artists, and it was probably right to say that the family was interested in signing with him. His offer was fair, maybe not as high as some, but hardly an insult, either. And they knew he'd do all he could to help them along. Obviously, at eleven and ten, the boys couldn't sign any contracts for themselves, but after a family discussion it was all agreed—the Moffatt Brothers would sign with Polydor and work with Robert Byrne again. Friendship sometimes counted for a lot more than money. Frank and Darlana signed on the dotted line, and it was a done deal. The boys were going to make a record!

It also gave them a remarkable distinction. They became the youngest country band ever to sign a contract with a major American label. That in itself made them newsworthy. All those shows they'd played, both in Canada and America, had paid off handsomely. Being cute, and also being very good, meant that the big time might well be beckoning for them.

With a contract in hand, it was time to start looking for a place to live in Nashville, since it was going to be their new home. After a little looking, they found a house in a nice suburb, with a yard where the boys could play, a place where they could set things up exactly the way they wanted, with a good kitchen for home-cooked meals. One thing that Bob, Dave, Scott, and Clint had to get used to again was doing chores. They weren't performing most days any more, so there was more time. Frank and Darlana could

THE MOFFATTS

have enrolled them in school, but by now they'd all become so used to home schooling that it made sense to continue. And, looking ahead, once the record was released, they'd be on the road, so it would be home schooling then, anyway. The only downside was that the boys didn't get to mix so much with kids their own age. But at least there were kids in the neighborhood, and the boys soon made some friends to hang with and enjoy life as just boys, not musicians.

Their days were still highly ordered, with school, instrument practice, working on songs for the record. The first thing to do was make demos of the songs, and see how they sounded with some rough recording, whittling down the number. Then it was into pre-production, working up arrangements, hiring the players, selecting the studio. Every aspect of it was new to the boys, and every moment was fascinating. After all, they'd made a huge leap. Saying you'd played in Branson or Vegas was one thing. Saying you were making a record for a major label was something else, especially if you were eleven or ten. Then it was a very big deal indeed. It made them very different from most other kids whose lives were limited by school, family, and the neighborhood. The Moffatts had already done things other kids just dreamed about. Now, everyone hoped, they were going to be stars.

Thirty or forty years ago, a band could make a whole album in a day, taping song after song. Those days had long since passed. More recently, it wasn't unusual for one or two songs to be completed in a three-hour studio session. But those days were history, too. Now it was all about perfection, and that took a long time. You didn't make an album in a week, or even a month. It was a long, involved process where the producer was as important as the artist. Most records took months to make. Not that every day was used for recording; far from it. It happened in bits and pieces, often in several different studios. The labels were investing a lot of money in each record, and they wanted every one to be a potential winner. That was the name of the game. So although the boys were eager to just have it done, to have the CD out so they could hold it in their hands and see it in the stores, they had to be patient.

Perhaps the best news was that the family would have some of their own songs on the record. They'd played some for Byrne, and a few had impressed him. But they were most proud of "Don't Judge This Book," which would become the final cut.

"We wrote this song for kids who may not feel like they fit in," explains Clint, "and it's also about handicapped people. We think handicapped people are just like us in their hearts, and it's not fair to treat them any differently."

It was a good sentiment, and an even better song, and it made the final cut, although it would end up being their only composing credit on the record. Still, it was a start.

It was good that Byrne was taking the boys' songwriting seriously. But then, from the beginning, anyone who'd seen them work knew they had to take them seriously.

"In the business, all the adults we've been around have always treated us just like other bands, with respect," Bob points out.

The Moffatts, as the record would be called, was a record guaranteed to get respect, even if it seemed like forever before it came out—it wouldn't hit the stores until June of 1995, four years to the month before the reinvented Moffatts released *Chapter 1: A New Beginning* in the U.S.

This being the video age, with channels like TNN and CMT happily airing country music videos, the boys had to do one of their own. Well, not just once, actually, but three—"Caterpillar Crawl," "Guns of Love," and "I Think She Likes Me." It was an indication of the faith Polydor (and most specifically Robert Byrne) had in them that the label would bankroll three videos without even waiting to see how the album was selling. In fact, they did even more than that. They also shot footage of the boys at home, and took old home movies of the boys, put it all together with the songs, and released it commercially as a home video when the CD appeared. That was faith. But then again, over the last couple of years, the boys had entertained a lot of people, both in Branson and Las Vegas, people who'd remember their names, and who might well want to buy their CD and video.

Of course, most of the material on the album came from outside writers. There was even a cover of a Garth Brooks song, "When God Made You," which was an indicator of the general new direction being given to the band—something a bit younger, a bit more commercial. After all, the aim was to sell records, and this being country music, the audiences wanted the styles they liked and were familiar with, nothing radically different; radically different didn't play well in this field.

The months of recording had been good for the family in many ways. As musicians, the boys had enjoyed a real lesson in how to put a record together, what worked and didn't work in terms of arrangements and songs. Hearing themselves constantly on studio playbacks had forced them to really sharpen their harmonies. But they'd become professionals, and they were willing and able to put in the work to make it all happen.

Going home, to a real home, every night, had been wonderful for everybody. It was a place that was theirs, where they could relax, and really enjoy family life. The boys could go outside and play together or with the friends they'd made in the neighborhood, and Frank and Darlana could relax. Maybe it wasn't Victoria—Nashville could get as hot and humid as Branson in the summer—but it was a real home, with all their things around them. They were settled, and everyone was happy. Things couldn't have been going better.

Once Scott, Clint, Dave, and Bob had finished the recording, they were naturally eager for the CD to be out. In reality, though, recording was only the first stage in the process. After that, each song had to be mixed. That meant adjusting levels for all the instruments and voices (each of which was recorded on to a separate track) until it sounded just right. Then, when that was complete—a lengthy process that required listening to each cut again and again, often making minute alternations—it had to be mastered. That took place in a special studio, with an engineer doing even more tinkering to try and make the sound as perfect as it could be. Nor was that the very last thing. After that the business end became involved. There was an album cover to be designed, photos of the band had to be taken, and just the right ones selected, and the songs on the CD had to be sequenced. There was an art to that, too, starting off with something very strong to make the casual listener keep on listening, then keeping just the right mood all the way to the end, closing with something equally strong to stick in people's memories and make them want to play it again and again.

Finally, the people at the label had to pick the right time to release the disc. If it was a busy time of year, a debut by a new group could easily get lost among the big names. And there had to be plenty of publicity and public appearances, as well as radio airplay, so people would know the album was out there in the stores. The Moffatts had to contend with all of that, and wait until just the right time, hard as that was to do. They just had to believe it would be worthwhile.

And it was. The record kicked off with "I Think She Likes Me," which was very pop-country. To anyone coming to the early Moffatts from their rock work, it would be a shock, hearing just how high their voices were back then. There was Scott's lead vocal, with the others supporting him with strong harmonies, while Nashville session men provided the musical backing (as they would throughout the album).

"This Boy" was a cover of the Beatles song written by Lennon and McCartney, given a much more country treatment than its composers had ever imagined. It gave full rein to the boys' harmonies, which really were superb. Again, it was Scott who was mixed ahead of the others, but without his brothers, the track would have sounded very empty.

The third cut, "Guns of Love," was one of the real standouts. It actually had nothing to do with guns, but everything to do with the battle of the sexes. It was a pretty major production, opening with military style drums and a keyboard imitating bagpipes. The chorus was a killer, but the verse, featuring Scott, was what put it over the top, impossible to resist.

"Mama Never Told Me 'Bout You," had a much bluesier feel to it, and its lyric, about what a mother had told the singer, was actually perfect for a boy to sing. The song got a groove and just stuck to it. And the "bop-bop" backing on the chorus was a stroke of genius.

The collection of strong material continued with "Just Thinkin' About You." It was obvious that the South had affected Scott—all you needed to do was hear his accent when he sang; he sounded as if he'd been born in Tennessee, rather than just moved there a few months before. As the title implied, this was a love song, and it might have seemed odd for a bunch of pre-teens to be singing that, but they made it work—in a lighthearted fashion.

"When God Made You," of course, was the song Garth Brooks had co-written with Pat Alger. Opening with just Scott's voice backed by acoustic guitar, it filled out. When the other brothers joined in on the chorus, they turned the tune into something genuinely moving and very special. It certainly helped that it was also one of the better songs Brooks had written, up to that point.

It was intense, and after that, a little light relief was needed, which was exactly what "Caterpillar Crawl" offered. Intended as the new line-dance song, it never quite managed that. The vocal effects that opened it all were rather weird, but it soon took off into straight cute. It might well have succeeded as a novelty number, and it certainly was part of the boys' live set, one that always got people dancing, but it never quite became the hit everyone hoped.

"You Are What You Do," was one of those songs that stood as good advice in its lyrics, and it was certainly true. You do bad things, you're a bad person. You do good things, you're a good person. It was a mid-tempo boogie that burst into a pure country chorus—probably the most country song on the entire album. More than anything, it showed just how strong a vocalist Scott was, one who had to be taken seriously by anyone who heard him. The same was true of his brothers, whenever those natural harmonies burst out.

Keeping up the tempo, "A Little Something," started off like swamp-pop before getting beat-happy. While not the best song on *The Moffatts*, it did really give everyone a chance to shine on the chorus.

"Don't Judge This Book" was *the* special song to the guys, and not just because they'd written it with Frank. It was more the message it put across, and the way someone perceived as different or an outsider was really just a regular person. It was a slow ballad, and, curiously, featured less of the harmonies than other tracks—the triplets didn't even come in until the second verse. But once the four voices were working together, the magic was sublime. And it was an impassioned piece of writing, too.

And that was it. Their first major-label album, and probably less "country" than many people expected. There was still a lot of pop on there, showing the first sign for their future direction, even if no one was even vaguely thinking of that yet. Scott stood out as a great singer, one who could do a lot with a lyric, and if the album didn't quite do justice to the other brothers' contribution, their harmonies were still naturally marvelous. Given the fact that *The Moffatts* would go on to sell some 300,000 copies, obviously a lot of people liked the sound, too. For now, however, it was time to think about getting the show back on the road.

Performing live had always been what they did, at least until now. It was what they knew, and with what they'd learned in the studio, they could bring a whole lot more to the stage now. Almost a year had passed since they'd performed, and the boys were anxious to get back to it—it was the longest time they'd been away from the stage since they'd begun in 1989, some six years earlier.

THE MOFFATTS

Scott was twelve, the others eleven; it seemed impossible that they could have crammed so much experience into so few years. But they had, and now they were eager to be back on the road, doing the thing they enjoyed most in life—singing. So it was with a sense of joy and relief that they found themselves rehearsing hard again, working with a band, all seasoned musicians, working on the songs from the record, plus others, to play live.

The record label's publicists had been working hard to give the record a real push. Apart from press and radio, the real focus was going to be on television. The fact that the brothers were so young, and decidedly cute, even at that age, worked in their favor, and plenty of TV gigs were lined up for June of 1995, when the record would finally hit the stores. Once it was out, they could really get moving and back on the road, with a summer full of bookings—their first American tour.

The television shows covered the whole spectrum. It wasn't a medium that was completely new to them, since, during their stints in Branson and Las Vegas, they'd become a favorite of Ralph Emery, who'd featured them on his *Nashville Now* show a remarkable fourteen times! But they'd never been on anything as big as *Good Morning America* or *Sally Jessy Raphael*, which was where they were headed this time around. Nationally broadcast by the networks, it meant they'd been seen by huge numbers of people all over the country, helping to make a massive audience aware of just who they were, even before they went on tour.

Naturally, the boys were nervous at first, but once they got the chance to sing, all the nerves were forgotten. This was what they were all about, and they came across fantastically. You didn't think of them as kids, but real performers—in other words, exactly what they were.

Aimed at a more country audience, they were also featured on *Wildhorse Saloon*, a show on The Nashville Network, which gave them a chance to reach the people who'd be among the most likely to go out and buy their album.

But that wasn't the limit of their TV appearances. As they crossed the country, there were any number of appearances on local television magazine programs, all of which helped to promote the record and their appearances.

Even with a major label record, they still weren't hitting the concert halls, not even as an opening act. Instead, they were hitting the ordinary people right where they lived, with appearances at the state and county fairs which were happening all over during the summer, and also at malls—exactly where they'd be likely to find kids who might get into them, and also more families.

This was reality, this was what they knew and loved, and after so much time away from it, they performed with a vengeance, giving it their all on every appearance. Now they were real recording artists; they definitely had something to prove, that they could be taken as seriously as anyone else out there. More than that, it gave them the opportunity to establish a whole new fan base. There'd be people who'd picked up on the record after hearing songs on the radio, and who'd come to see them. And then there'd be people who were just passing by, stopped to listen, and who might go out and purchase their album later (the family carried copies with them to sell after every show, the way most artists do). Just as they'd done in Canada, then in Branson and Las Vegas, they were making converts one by one.

At the same time, they had a very realistic attitude about it all.

"We love to make music," Scott says. "People have to understand that if we're going to be able to keep on making music, we have to sell records because that's what keeps the money coming in—we have to make money, too, because it's a normal job . . . we have to sell records, we have to tour constantly."

It felt great to be on the road again, and it gave them a major opportunity to see America. They knew three cities, and while they'd passed through other places, most of the country was a mystery to them. This way they got to know it very well, going from cities to small towns, hitting both the back roads and the interstates, meeting people where they lived and played and shopped—the real America. Sure, every night was a different motel that ended up seeming the same, and meals were taken in restaurants, diners, and coffee shops, but after so long away from it, that all seemed thrilling again.

And the thrills just kept coming and coming. In July they were up in Connecticut, at the Special Olympics, which were being held there. The Moffatt brothers formed part of the country entertainment, which included The Pointer Sisters, Tracy Byrd, and Michelle Wright, the Canadian country the boys all remembered seeing on television a few years before, and one of their inspirations. They got to sing "Don't Judge This Book" to an audience that would fully understand its meaning—the type of people for whom they'd written it; it was an emotional high point of the summer.

But the summer of 1995 contained so many high points it was hard to keep track of them all. They were invited to sing the National Anthem at a number of sporting events—quite odd, considering that "The Star-Spangled Banner" wasn't even *their* anthem, since they were Canadian. One time they even got to sing it before an early season game of the Dallas Cowboys, who just happened to be the boys' favorite team.

There were enough gigs, and offers of gigs, to keep them on the road for months—which was just fine with the boys. They'd enjoyed being settled in Nashville, but this was what they loved, entertaining the crowds. However, Frank and Darlana insisted on frequent breaks; they didn't want anyone (including themselves) getting burned out, and they didn't want the boys to forget that they had a home. Keeping that base and being there often was important to remembering just who they were, rather than simply becoming a music machine.

Still, it was gratifying that so many people and places wanted to book them, and their datebook was full into the spring of 1996—an enviable position for any group of musicians, let alone one with their first album not long out. Once the fair season ended, they'd be concentrating on malls. For country acts it was unconventional; but it seemed to work; they continued to draw crowds wherever they appeared, and television and radio shows were happy to have them as guests. Not only could they sing, but the boys were polite and articulate, as genuinely nice as could be.

During the fall came a special television offer, to appear on Riders in the Sky's Christmas special, *Rider Theater Christmas*. Since 1987 Riders in the Sky—the band consisting of Ranger Doug, Woody Paul, and Too Slim, had been cult favorites for the way they paid tribute to (and also gently poked fun at) the B-movie cowboy songs from the Forties and Fifties. In 1987 they'd released *Riders Radio Theater*, which led to them doing a program of the same name on National Public Radio, and in the early Nineties they'd briefly had a Saturday morning show on CBS. *Rider Theater Christmas* wasn't part of any new series, it was simply a Christmas show starring the band, which would air on TNN. But it was acknowledgment from the band the boys had watched on Saturday mornings. That fact made it all the more special than the television they'd done promoting their record.

CHAPTER 5

But they had a Christmas record of their own, albeit not an official release. It was a cassette, available only through the Moffatts' fan club in Nashville—and it was a sign of success that they'd been forced to start a fan club—of the Moffatt brothers singing Christmas songs, some old, some new—and some not so serious. The track listing was "Old Man Winter," "The Brightest Stat," "Earl the Christmas Squirrel," "The Greatest Gift," "Santa's in My Neighborhood," "How Would Jesus Feel," "Oh What a Wonderful Day," "Santa Knows," "Christmas Eve," "Santa Left a Hole in Daddy's Pocket."

Making a Christmas tape as a thank-you to the fans (and also as something extra to sell at seasonal shows) made perfect sense. Going back to Elvis Presley, fan clubs had handled Christmas records; it was something of a tradition. And who better to do a Christmas record than four boys for whom the season was still quite magical? And just because it wasn't made for Polydor didn't mean it wasn't professionally done. By now the guys had a real handle on things. It certainly hadn't cost as much to make as their "real" album, but there was nothing amateurish about it—they had their reputation to maintain! The cassette (which is still available from the Moffatts fan club) did give them a chance to release more of their own compositions, however. They'd been eager to do that since they'd been writing more. Even on the road, they spent time every day practicing their instruments—if they were going to become good, daily practice, even when they didn't want to do it, was the only way. And there was definite instrumental talent. They might never be Nashville session musicians, but they were way above adequate. They'd even begun to play on stage a little, although most of the work was done by their band, who'd now settled into their roles behind the brothers. But the playing in front of people did give them a new goal to strive for, to become good enough to become mostly self-contained. For the moment, however, that was unlikely. Scott was still only twelve, and the others eleven; there was a limit to the responsibility they could handle.

Just after the holidays, they were approached about the possibility of appearing with the Statler Brothers on television. The Statler Brothers (who weren't brothers, and none of whom was named Statler) hosted a variety show on TNN, and toured, although they hadn't released too many records in recent years, but they'd had their fair share in a career that had lasted thirty years. In fact, that was what this particular program was celebrating—their thirtieth anniversary. A three-CD compilation of their best work had been issued, and the program promised to be something special. The Statler Brothers had always specialized in vocal harmony work—not unlike the Moffatt brothers. And that comparison would work well, since they wanted the Moffatts to appear as the young Statler Brothers—although it's doubtful that the Statlers were quite *that* young when they began—singing one of their hits, "Class of '57," which had hit the country charts in 1972, eleven years before Scott was born. Of course, it was an honor to be asked, and they gladly performed for the cameras.

The program aired in March of 1996, which proved to be a big month for Scott, Clint, Dave, and Bob. Not only did they celebrate their birthdays then, moving to thirteen and twelve, respectively, but they were also nominated for the TNN/MCN Award for Best Vocal Group of the Year. That put them in auspicious company in country music circles, and it was true to say that simply to be nominated was an honor. They didn't win, but they hadn't expected to. Just seeing their name there was a massive boost. But perhaps not as big as something that happened at the end of the month: they were invited to perform at no less a place than the White House!

A few years before they'd appeared at Parliament Hill, in Ottawa, Canada, and played there. But even in their wildest dreams they'd never expected an invitation to the White House. After all, as Frank and Darlana kept reminding them, they were Canadians, not Americans, and there were plenty of American groups who could have been asked.

It was the day of the annual Easter Egg Roll and Hunt, an event aimed, obviously, at kids, and the Moffatts had made their names as one of the leading groups of young entertainers in the country; it was a perfect fit. They got to meet President and Mrs. Clinton, as well as their daughter Chelsea, and to entertain the parents and children who'd been chasing Easter eggs on the White House lawn. There was also a tour of the residence, including areas most visitors never got to see. In a life that was already totally crammed with events, this was definitely one to remember.

Back in Canada, the Moffatts had got their first break by playing the Easter Seals telethon. Ever since then they'd performed charity work, like their appearance at the Special Olympics in 1995. They didn't make a big deal out of it; it was simply a part of their lives. Fate had been very kind to them, and this was an opportunity to give something back to those who'd been less fortunate than themselves. They were happy to appear at fundraisers, and lend their name to good causes, and they were actively involved with D.A.R.E., Feed the Children (a cause very close to their hearts, still being young themselves), and The Rainforest Foundation, making appearances for all three in the spring of 1996.

One of the questions that would have to be asked soon was what would happen after the brothers' voices broke. They could all sing wonderfully now, but there was no guarantee that would be the case later. And while their voices were breaking, what should they do? It would be an odd period, when they'd have little control over what their voices did, sometimes going from high to low and back again in the space of one sentence. It was a tough time for boys, and for those who made their living singing it would be especially difficult. They could record while their voices broke, but touring would be hard, if not impossible. And, depending on how things went, it could be the end of the Moffatts as a vocal harmony group. To be fair, it hadn't happened yet, but it would, within the next couple of years, and everyone, particularly the boys, had to be prepared for what might happen.

And there was something else the brothers had to be prepared for. Frank and Darlana had tried to hide it from them, but in all likelihood they hadn't succeeded. The family spent so much time together that hiding anything would probably have been impossible. The truth was that the two of them weren't getting along too well, and were contemplating a separation and possibly divorce.

It was something that happened in many families, but Scott, Clint, Bob, and Dave had never thought it could happen to *them*. Nor had Frank and Darlana. But circumstances change, sometimes love dies, sometimes other factors enter the picture to end a relationship. It wasn't as if they didn't know each other well—they'd been married for almost a decade and a half, after all. They both loved their boys, and they continued to want the very best for them. Going back, Darlana had had a promising singing career herself, and she'd put it aside to help guide the boys. Now they were established, she wanted to return to her own singing, before it became too late. She wasn't old, by any means, but she knew that in the business there was a limited amount of time in which you could make it, and she wanted her shot. By now she had the contacts in Nashville, and she knew she had the talent.

Frank, who'd sung himself, then given up, was content

THE MOFFATTS

to look after his sons. Managing them had become a full-time job, looking after their bookings, traveling with them, taking care of many, many different things all connected with the Moffatts. He and Darlana had already agreed that if they split up permanently, he'd look after the boys while she pursued her dream.

They'd still see their mother, of course—she was their mom, after all—but it wouldn't be every day, the way they'd been used to. She wouldn't hit the road with them, share everything with them. For the boys, as for any kids, it was a major shock. Even if they'd known, if they'd seen it coming, they'd managed to deny it, until their parents sat them down and explained it to them.

Things would change, inevitably. For a while, absolutely nothing would seem the same, and everyone would feel lost, Frank and Darlana as much as their kids. But sometimes the hardest decisions to make could turn out for the best. If the marriage wasn't working, it wasn't fair on anyone to stay together. They'd still see each other, remain friends—they had too much time invested, and knew each other too well not to be friends—and they'd share the boys. Darlana would be proud of what her sons had achieved, and would achieve in the future, and she hoped she'd have her own career they could take pride in, too. It was a parting of the ways, but that didn't mean the road had ended. But it might be a little while before the boys and their father got back up to speed again.

Music became the constant in their lives, the thing that kept them going. It had been a part of them all for so long that it was now their rock, while the rest of the boys' world was falling apart. They'd always been taught that as professionals, they had to put on a good show, and that was what they continued to do. It just seemed weird to be out on the road without their mother there, and even stranger to return to Nashville and not have her around all the time. But that was the way it was going to have to be from now on, and they needed to get used to it.

To make matters worse, they were finding more time on

their hands. The long stretch of touring in support of their record was coming to a close, which meant a lot less time traveling around America. There were still shows, but nowhere near as many, and mostly closer to home.

The Moffatts hadn't been a chart hit, which was a disappointment to the family, who'd all truly believed in it. They'd certainly done everything they could to make it into a success, and in the end, even without being a hit, it still sold a remarkable 300,000 copies. So it certainly hadn't been a complete loser, either, and Robert Byrne, the vice-president who'd signed them to their contract, still had faith in them. The problem was that their label was going out of business, and it was debatable what would happen to the acts. Some might go to other Polydor labels, and some might be let go.

It wasn't exactly what Frank and his sons wanted to hear. Sales of *The Moffatts* had been more than respectable, and they'd made a lot of new friends when they were touring. What they'd done was build a fan base, and in some ways that was better than becoming an overnight sensation. Acts who've toured and established their fan bases usually last a lot longer than those who came from nowhere, enjoyed mega-sales, but didn't have the act or the material to follow it up. By 1996 the general feeling seemed to be release it all and see what sticks. The acts who didn't stick were very quickly, and very quietly, dropped. Being a musician had always been an insecure life. Now, it seemed, it was more insecure than ever.

Of course, they weren't failures, not by any definition. They'd released two albums, one on a major label, as well as a home video, and all had sold quite well, even if they hadn't charted. They were making a very good living from playing live. In any book, that was success, even if it didn't have the sweetness of a hit. Yes, life had changed about them—they were living in another country, and their parents had split up, but things did change. At heart, they were still the same guys they'd always been. When they were home in Nashville they still hung out with the other kids in the neighborhood, played soccer and football, watched hockey on television (one part of their Canadian past they'd never be able to let go of, and didn't want to—they still rooted for the Vancouver Canucks), and took classes in kung fu. They had normal lives. But there was also the home schooling with Frank, the rehearsals and time practicing their instruments, the things that made them different from all the other boys they knew—things that made them a lot cooler, in fact.

When all the dust settled from the closure of their label, the Moffatts found themselves without a record deal. That wasn't good news, by any means, but for right now it wasn't quite the end of the world, either. Life would go on. There was no shortage of concert dates, and there was always the possibility of a return to Branson or to Vegas, where the money was good and the hours very regular.

In fact, in some ways, it could have been a blessing in disguise. As Frank knew all too well, the boys were growing and changing every single day; he watched them, he couldn't help but notice. And it was apparent that they were all widening their tastes in music. Where they'd once just listened to country, now the radio was often set to an alternative station, and the sounds he'd hear when they were rehearsing and writing had very little to do with Nashville picking. That was fine. The more they heard, the more influences they took in, the more rounded their music and their songs would become. His boys still had plenty of faith in themselves, and he had a great deal of faith in them. In the end, everything would work out fine. They had talent, and they had persistence. With those two qualities, they couldn't help but be winners in the long run. The lines between country and pop were so blurred that it was sometimes impossible to know which was which, anyway. And they were willing to work hard for their success; they knew by now that it didn't come easily. They were survivors, and creative. Yes, at the end of the day they'd be just fine. . . .

PART TWO
THE NEW BEGINNING

CHAPTER 6

It was time for a very serious rethink. The Moffatts were without a record contract, and the boys seemed to be gradually moving away from country music. They had shows to play, which was something, and they could make a living. Maybe they could have returned to Branson or Vegas, but the boys were definitely not in favor of that. They were ready for a major musical upheaval.

To them, this couldn't have happened at a better time, odd as that might sound. But it was true. They were growing up, and their tastes were changing. Scott was fourteen, and the others were thirteen. They'd discovered a musical world that extended way beyond country, and they were eager to be a part of it. What they were listening to now seemed to speak directly to them, to move them. As Scott says, "Well, before our influences were people like Dwight Yoakam, Garth Brooks, and stuff like that because we played country music, and at the time when we made our transition, it was more like Nirvana, the Beatles, and Bush."

That transition was still very tentative, however, and tending to take place only when the boys were rehearsing, practicing their instruments, or working at their songwriting. It was something that was bubbling under more than breaking through, since there was still a living to be made playing country, and the guys knew instinctively that the two styles wouldn't mix on stage. When the dates that were booked were over, *then* they could concentrate on the future.

There were other changes going on in the family, too. Frank had been dating a woman named Sheila for a few months. She was a dental assistant, and thirty-one years old. From the way things were going, it was apparent that it was pretty serious. It was one step at a time, but the boys were beginning to understand that she might become their new stepmother. Not that she'd attempt to replace their mom, whom they saw regularly, since she, too, lived in Nashville. But it made the whole period feel like one of transition.

Finally all the dates were fulfilled, and Frank sat down to talk to his sons—or, more accurately, to listen to what they had to say. It wasn't that they wanted to give up. It wasn't that they disliked country—it was their roots—but they wanted to move away from it, into something new, something different, something that expressed who they really were.

The Beatles had made the statements for Frank's generation. They'd changed the entire course of popular music, and in doing so, become the biggest band in the world, keeping that stature even thirty years after they'd broken up. They'd redefined the idea of a pop song, grown from album to album, and pushed down all kinds of musical barriers. They remained the source for all pop bands, whether directly or indirectly.

Nirvana's success had come in the early Nineties, with the album *Nevermind*, and the single "Smells like Teen Spirit." Originally from Aberdeen, Washington, they relocated to Seattle, brought in a new drummer, and things really took off in 1991. Classed by many as grunge, it was really the alienation in Kurt Cobain's lyrics and voice that reached out and touched a generation of teenagers who hadn't had anyone to speak for them before. They seemed to shoot from unknown to superstars, with Cobain suddenly wearing a crown he hadn't asked for and didn't want. The pressure of fame, among other things, proved to be too much for him, and in April 1994 he committed suicide. In death he seemed to become even larger than life, and his music lived on.

Bush, however, were a different case altogether. Much of their sound seemed to be based on another Seattle band, Pearl Jam. Bush were from Britain, but their sound was completely American, heavily influenced, apart from Pearl Jam, by the other bands who'd emerged from the Seattle scene, including Nirvana. The single "Everything Zen" helped break them, and their first album sold well. Leader Gavin Rossdale was incredibly photogenic, which certainly didn't hinder the situation. But while they certainly sounded commercial, there wasn't much originality in their music.

One thing was certain: What the Moffatts were looking for was a sound that was much heavier, and more modern than the music they'd been playing. It would be more aggressive. But in all the years they'd been singing and writing, they'd learned the value of a good melody and a strong chorus, and those weren't lessons they were about to forget.

They'd also been very lucky. By now all of their voices had broken, and they'd all come through being able to sing well. That all four of them should have made it that way was sheer luck. But it had happened—and that had to be a good sign for the future, didn't it?

The Beatles, Nirvana, and Bush formed the bases of what was changing in the Moffatts' sound. But, listening to the radio, it was impossible for them to be unaware of a few other things, such as the ska-influenced music of bands like No Doubt and the Mighty Mighty Bosstones, and it was only natural that they should incorporate some of that feel, too.

One thing, obviously, was that the boys didn't feel in the least bit alienated by the world. Why would they? Life had been good to them, really. They'd spent the last few years doing something they loved, and they'd been very well paid for it. They'd seen all of the U.S. and Canada, they'd put out records—by most standards, their life had been a fairy tale.

There was one big drawback to all these changes they were making, however. It put them right back to square one. The country audiences wouldn't want to hear what they wanted to play, and no pop audience had ever heard of them—not that there was really an equivalent pop circuit they could play. They were back to being unknowns again, just like starting over.

Still, there were worse fates. They were starting over with knowledge, contacts, and a proven track record. According to Frank's books, the Moffatts had already played more than twelve hundred shows in their professional career—an impressive figure, given their ages.

Before they could go any further, though, the first thing they had to do was solidify their direction. Talking about it, and playing a little was one thing. Writing songs that reflected where they were heading was another thing altogether—particularly writing a bunch of very strong songs. That was the next order of business, with the brothers working together, pooling their ideas, having equal input, and then making tapes of them on the small machine they had at home to listen to and criticize later, then go back and improve.

For once, there was little Frank could do to help. This was the boys really asserting their independence, growing up and growing away, the way all children do. The timing was good. He and Sheila had just married, and were going through changes and adjustments of their own, learning to live together, still in the honeymoon period of their relationship.

For Sheila, it was particularly hard. She was entering an established and tightly knit family. Frank and the boys had an unusual relationship, spending as much time together as they did. She wasn't trying to replace Darlana, simply to be accepted, and hopefully loved by the brothers for who she was. She had skills with makeup that might prove useful to them in future public appearances, and, at thirty-one, she was young enough to relate to a lot of the music they'd started listening to (she'd been born the year before Kurt Cobain).

Since the boys had had a chance to know her before she married Frank, things went relatively smoothly. They got on with their lives and their music, still being schooled at home every day, hanging out with their buds, going to see their mom.

Perhaps the biggest thing was the excitement that Scott, Clint, Dave, and Bob all felt. All the change was good, it was what they needed in their lives to shake things up a bit and make it all happen all over again. Their writing was beginning to take on a focus, and all the time they'd spent practicing their instruments was really beginning to pay off in a big way. For the first time they really felt in control of what they were doing, that they were the ones calling the shots. If it all took off, the credit would be all theirs, and if it failed, well, there'd be no one else to blame. But that was fine. It would all stand and fall on what they did.

Something they couldn't know right then was that very slowly, there was a groundswell of teenage music happening. For the most part, it was taking off in Germany and Asia, with boy bands like the Backstreet Boys and 'N Sync finding an audience. Granted, what they were doing was very different from the Moffatts, but it proved that teens wanted to listen to teens.

And closer to home, there was Hanson.

They hadn't really hit it big yet, but things were moving along. After being rejected by fourteen record companies who couldn't see their potential, Mercury had finally signed them, and was willing to take the risk, which would, of course, pay off in a massive way. Of course, the Moffatts had never heard of Hanson, but the fact that they existed and had been signed by a major label was known in the industry. Again, it was a part of that teen wave that would break over America in 1998.

Meanwhile, just working completely on their own, unaware of any of this, the brothers were writing songs, and refining others they'd completed. The great thing about operating in a new field was that there were no rules. They could do whatever they wanted, and just follow their instincts, and that was exactly what they did. They were having *fun*, the time of their lives.

When they were finally ready for Frank to hear them, they'd been working non-stop on their new material for a couple of months, and had a tape with several songs. Their studio experience, as well as working on equipment at home, meant they knew how to put together a fairly polished demo tape, and that's what they gave their father.

When he sat down and listened to it a few times, Frank Moffatt was impressed. He thought he knew what his sons were capable of, but this astonished him. Not just the way they'd come on as musicians, but also the quality of their writing. They hadn't just copied the bands they'd been listening to, they'd taken the sounds and created something new and very fresh. More than that, it was something, he believed, that could be very commercial. The boys might have just found their future.

As the band's manager, it was his job to wonder what might be the best place for them. Simply looking at the charts, it was apparent that America wasn't yet ready for teen bands—this was the middle of 1997, after all. But Europe had always seemed receptive to that, although they'd never been confronted by a teen rock band before, just singers. Maybe that would work, he thought. Go to another country, where no one knew the brothers as a country act, and make a fresh start, see how it all worked.

Of course, to succeed in pop music, they'd need a record. But he could see that the boys were itching to get back into the studio anyway. Their tape was good and strong, it gave a great indication of what they could do and where they were going. It was time to find the new Moffatts a record contract!

Frank didn't even try the American labels—at that point he figured he'd simply be wasting his breath, and he'd have been right. No one would have taken him seriously, even

Mercury, since Hanson had still to prove themselves.

Even England, which had always loved teen-oriented bands, didn't show any interest, much to his surprise. But they seemed to like their idols singing, not playing. So there was no choice but to start looking farther afield, and that was what he began to do. One company that showed some interest was the German division of music giant EMI. Teen bands did even better in Germany than in England—it was where both the Backstreet Boys and 'N Sync would first break—and they loved Americans. The Moffatts weren't American, obviously, but to most Germans they might as well have been.

One thing was beyond doubt—what the brothers were doing was completely different. Unlike other teen bands, they weren't just singing to backing musicians or a tape. They could be self-contained. And they wrote a lot of their own material. There had been no one like them aimed at a teen audience in years. In part, that was because the face of music had changed with the growth of R&B and hip-hop. Singers, not instrumentalists, had become the vogue. So that was in their favor.

All they needed was a chance to prove themselves, and after a lot of talk, EMI Germany was willing to give them that. They'd pay for the band to go into the studio in New York with a producer, and put out a single, promote it, and once it had performed well, there'd be an album, and EMI or its associated companies around the world would release it. There was going to be a major push, with lots of promotion.

Frank breathed a sigh of relief, and the boys were ecstatic. Now they could show everyone what they could really do.

Recording in New York was vastly different to Nashville. The pace of the city, always so fast, seemed to dictate the way things were run. Nashville was all business, too, but in a more Southern, laid-back way. This was rush, rush, rush, so daunting to everyone. Both Frank and the boys felt a little intimidated—at least until they began to play. Then there was a sense of control, of doing what they did well, of working with the producer, rather than for him. Unlike Robert Byrne, this producer was an outsider, someone who didn't really have anything vested in their success. They had to prove themselves to him first, to win him over.

It was hard work in the studio; there was no doubt about that. The days were as long as the law allowed for minors, but the sounds that were coming out simply energized Clint, Dave, Bob, and Scott. The music was electric in more ways than one. There were backing tracks, lead tracks, lead vocals, backing vocals, overdubs. It was wearying, but still exciting, and after every take they'd listen to the playback, certain within themselves that this was going to work, and willing do anything to make sure it happened.

After the tracks had been mixed, they were even better than the guys had hoped. They were both pop and rock, a couple of them not a million miles from Bryan Adams, their Canadian countryman who'd been a huge star for well over a decade, and whom Clint sometimes cited as one of their influences. His sound might have been a bit more mainstream than theirs, but the success he'd enjoyed was undeniable (even in '99 Adams still enjoys hits, having just had a British top ten single, a duet with Mel C. of the Spice Girls).

While most of the songs they'd recorded had been written by outsiders, the brothers had managed to tape a couple they'd written (with help from Frank). Really, though, what they wanted were the songs that best captured the sound they were after, no matter who'd penned them, and two of the best, "I'll Be There for You" and "I Miss You Like Crazy" had come from the team of Brunner and Coplan. They had a real punch, something that came across incredibly well. After listening, the record company agreed, and "I'll Be There for You" was selected as the single, to appear late in October, before the Christmas rush.

That meant the family would be spending a lot of time

in Germany—essentially the next several months. They'd be on television, in magazines, and most of all, they'd be touring, building up a fan base for the new Moffatts. Rather than spend all their time in hotels and motels, it just made sense to move there for a while. It was a major leap, picking up and transporting themselves to a country where they didn't even speak the language in the hope of becoming pop stars. But if you didn't take a risk, you'd never get the payoff. Besides, what did they have to lose? Right now, musically, there was nothing in America, or even Canada, for them.

The boys were stoked about it, but they weren't the ones looking after all the details. That would come down to Frank and Sheila, who'd probably find the transition harder than Scott, Bob, Dave, or Clint. They understood just how much was riding on this. If it failed, then the Moffatts' musical career was effectively over, and they'd be stuck more than five thousand miles from home. But it was better not to think about failure. They were going to succeed!

As they had before, it was a case of going through everything, and deciding what to take and what to store. Given the distance, and the expense of moving, most everything went into storage—only the essentials would be making the trip across the Atlantic. The record company had arranged the renting of a house—furnished, of course—in the small town of Pulheim-Strommeln, some ten miles northwest of Cologne, in the middle section of the country, not far from the borders of Belgium and Holland.

It was little more than a village really. Apart from the houses, there were two churches, a few bars, and one supermarket. If you wanted something, you had to travel into Cologne to buy it. But Pulheim-Strommeln did have something the Moffatts would find useful—a recording studio. Dierks Studios had played host to German bands like the Scorpions and Die Toten Hosen, and, according to Scott, "even Michael Jackson secretly did a song here."

Being relatively isolated, and currently unused, the studio was ideal. The boys could go in and rehearse every day without disturbing anyone. And rehearse they most certainly would. Frank had a routine organized for them. They'd be up at seven-thirty each morning, go running, and then at nine they'd enter the studio, working until two, after which they'd have school. It made for long days, but they were used to those.

By the time they arrived in Germany, "I'll Be There For You" had been released, and had already entered the charts at number forty-six. They'd already been featured, both in pictures and in articles, in the teen magazines, but, Scott says, they were still astonished that "when we first set foot here, we were already recognized and asked for autographs."

It seemed like a good omen for the future. So did the house, which stood just outside the village, down a low, curving driveway, closed off from the rest of the world by a white gate. A statue of the Madonna sat in the front yard. The house was a single story, comfortably furnished. By all the standards they'd been used to in the States and Canada, though, it was like stepping back in time a little. In Europe, things still closed early, especially in the villages. There was no local equivalent of a 7-11, none of the conveniences they'd taken for granted all their lives. And, arriving in November from the relative warmth of Tennessee, the place seemed bone-chillingly cold.

But there was certainly nothing to distract them from the reason they'd come here, to put a new act together before going on tour. The one thing they'd decided was that they wouldn't be aloof with anyone who lived locally, and the locals went out of their way to make them feel welcome.

The single was continuing to rise up the charts. Reporters and television crews would come to the house to interview the guys, photo sessions would take place in the studio or the garden. They were happening. To most people it seemed like an overnight thing, but then they didn't know the whole Moffatts story. And even when they were told, they found it hard to believe that these kids could have been singing together for eight years; they just weren't old enough!

Actually, the Moffatt family wouldn't be in Germany that long, at least this time. A month after arriving, they'd be heading back to the States, to celebrate Christmas with Sheila's sister in Green Bay, Wisconsin (which in December would make western Germany seem like the Caribbean), then a trip back to Vancouver to visit grandparents, before a swing through Nashville, to catch up with their mom and some friends, before heading back to Pulheim-Strommeln, and three weeks of intense rehearsals, plus a few small shows.

The break would do them good, it would keep them grounded and in touch with their roots. Of course, it might not have been the best idea to leave Germany just as they were getting their first-ever chart success, but family came first; it always had and it always would.

The big test would come in 1998, when they began playing concerts. They'd come a long way as musicians, but was it far enough to hold a crowd? The rehearsals seemed to show that it was. Scott had developed into a natural front man, able to entertain. His hair had grown out, and he'd bleached the strands at the front, giving a two-tone look. Within the last year, all four brothers had really shot up. They'd grown tall and filled out a bit. It was hard to look at the cover of the first album and think these were the same people.

Of course, there would be those long-time fans who thought they'd sold out for leaving country music, but the simple fact was that you couldn't please everyone.

"Pop/rock is much more universal," Clint explains. "Country's not a well-known music everywhere." Without even really trying, the Moffatts had tapped into something that spoke to a lot of people in many different languages. You didn't even need to know the words to the songs—the feeling came across.

After just a month away, America seemed like a strange place. The way everything was so brightly lit, the commercial celebration of Christmas, it made them realize how low-key Germany really was, and how there was plenty of good and bad in both countries. Christmas itself was the quiet family occasion it had always been, with plenty of presents and singing, meeting their new aunt, and relaxing.

Vancouver was even better. It had been a long time since they'd lived in the Northwest, but it still felt like home, even after several years. The gray skies, the rain . . . it all came back to them. Vancouver was bigger and more cosmopolitan than ever, but Victoria barely seemed to have changed since they were kids there. It was like having a few days to walk around their own history, before catching a plane down to Nashville, to ring in the New Year with their mom, to see the friends they'd left a few weeks before, and get energized for the long flight back to Europe.

Once back in Germany, things would get really serious, making sure they had all the new songs completely down and ready to go. In the first stage of their career, all they'd had to do was sing. Now, all the weight was on them, and they had to be prepared for that. So it was a return to the daily grind, polishing each performance as they had in the studio, and even adding a cover song or two, like the Police's "Every Breath You Take."

There was a major gig ahead of them, their first in this new incarnation, at the *Bravo* Super Show in Dortmund, Germany, on February 6. *Bravo* was *the* German teen magazine, and they'd written extensively about the boys, individually and collectively, as their single was high in the charts. Before the Moffatts played such an important concert, though, they wanted the chance to perform before some smaller audiences, to work out the snags and problems that would inevitably occur.

To that end, they lined up a few small shows. It would give them a chance to get used to playing—as opposed to just singing—in public. It wasn't that they didn't have stage experience, just not the experience of doing it this way.

Interestingly, as all this was going on, back in the U.S. Hanson had broken through to the big time, on the basis of their big single "Mmm-Bop," and the album that followed, *Middle Of Nowhere*. While the two bands didn't exactly sound alike, it proved that there was a market for what the Moffatts were doing back in the United States, something which had to make them feel better. And when Hanson were interviewed on late-night television and gave thanks to the Moffatts for helping to show them that boys could make music, that was something of which they could really be proud.

The shows went off very smoothly, although the boys ended up changing one or two things in their act. For the most part, though, it was as they'd planned, and they made the trip to Dortmund ready to conquer the German teenagers with their music....

And that was exactly what they did. The country might have been mad for BSB and 'N Sync, but the Moffatts showed them there was a lot more going on musically. Clint and Bob formed a natural, solid rhythm section, while Scott could handle the guitar chores all too well on his Gibson Les Paul, with Dave on keys offering a foundation to it all. Not everything was electric, though. They could turn down the volume and all gather round to sing in close harmony, accompanied only by Scott's acoustic guitar for "I Miss You Like Crazy," which had already been picked as the next single, prior to the release of their album. They were impossible to resist, four guys, younger than the other bands who were playing, cute as could be, and who could play instruments, too. The crowd went crazy for them, and all of a sudden Moffet mania had really begun in Germany.

CHAPTER 7

They boys couldn't believe the ecstatic reception they received. It was as if the world had just gone crazy. They were happy to have gone over so well, but wondered if it could possibly be repeated. It could, and it was, as they played more dates around Germany. This was unlike anything they'd known in their country days, unlike anything they'd dreamed. The fans screamed for them, so loud that they could hardly hear themselves playing. In a way, though, it was disturbing, as if the fans couldn't be enjoying themselves, at least the ones who appeared to get *too* carried away, ending up in tears.

"If they're crying and stuff like that," Scott says, "I guess that's just a signal of their appreciation, although I would much rather see them just screaming and having a good time."

Being suddenly considered teen idols was new, and somewhat uncomfortable. To the brothers' minds, the only person to be worshiped was God, not themselves or any other human. And it took them awhile to accept that all these girls could really be getting wild about *them*. A few years before, that would have just seemed bizarre. But they'd grown up now, and they'd come to appreciate girls a lot more. Still, while many might have walked off the stages with swelled heads, that wasn't the case for the boys. They were first and foremost musicians. Anything else that

THE MOFFATTS

happened was just icing on the cake, as long as they were allowed to play the music they wanted.

The tour was scheduled to run for a month, while the new single came out—which of course went racing up the charts. Throughout Germany, and into Austria, and even staid Switzerland, the reactions from the audience were the same—they just loved the Moffatts and the music they were making. It was as if, after all the boy bands, the kids were primed and ready to rock out, and the Moffatts were giving them that release. Girls were doing everything they could to meet them, sneaking into theaters long before a show and hiding anywhere they could. Security quickly became a nightmare. They'd rapidly gone from zeros to heros, and Frank found himself having to hire a couple of bodyguards just to protect the boys!

Even when they returned to Pulheim-Strommeln, it wasn't to obscurity and peace and quiet. They'd made the mistake, on television, of telling people where they lived. Tracking them down from there was an easy matter for the fans.

"Every day there will be a group of fans waiting outside our house with their scrapbooks and pictures, asking for autographs," Sheila remembers. "On weekdays, there would be at least twenty, thirty of them. On the weekends, it can easily be about fifty to a hundred."

And these were dedicated fans. When the boys left home for the studio, the fans would jump on their bikes and ride over there, so they could ask for *more* autographs. It was unlike anything the brothers had ever imagined.

"When you walked on the stage and you hear all the fans screaming, it's a great feeling," Bob says. "And that people actually enjoy our music."

A second tour was hastily arranged—there was simply so much demand by the fans to be able to see the boys live. The album would be coming out in the summer, "I Miss You Like Crazy" was in the Top Ten, and the new edition of the Moffatts was an unqualified success. Still, the guys weren't thinking too much beyond playing.

"I mean, we really like the fact that the fans are appreciating what we are doing," Scott says. "But we never think about how much stardom we have or are going to have. The thing is to have as much fun as we can have doing what we are doing."

And obviously they'd struck a chord with a lot of people. But it was worth remembering that, apart from enjoying themselves, all the guys in the band were very serious musicians. Even when they were on tour, they practiced a minimum of two to three hours every day, sometimes as much as five or six—that was real dedication. Sometimes it would be going over tunes, making changes, working on new material. And sometimes it would just be jamming, playing for the fun of it, getting a chance to show off their chops on their instruments. That could be the most fun of all, playing just to entertain themselves. They'd have never done it in front of their fans, who'd come to hear them play songs. But just to let loose once in a while gave them all a real sense of freedom, always ending in big smiles and laughter.

They spent their birthdays on the road, and celebrated them there with parties. That was fine; they'd been on the road for birthdays before. Really, there was no place they'd have rather been. It was the way they'd begun their career, and it still gave them the biggest thrill. "We just want to do music and make people happy," Bob explains, and it sums up the Moffatts' philosophy.

They were still astonished, but totally stoked by the way things were going.

"The new sound has been great," Bob says. "We've been getting lots of air play."

That was an understatement. It seemed as if everywhere you went in Germany, the radio was playing a Moffatts song. And once the radio stations had advance copies of the album, they began airing cuts from that. The speed with which things had happened was just staggering, absolutely awesome. A year before they'd been dropped by their record label, and had been close to the end of a career. Now they were stars, bigger than they'd ever been. Country had been good to them for a long time, and had taught them a lot. But it looked as if pop music was going to treat them like kings.

The timing was right, but above all it was the music. Good pop music had never gone out of fashion with teens. But in the last couple of years, somehow the teen market had grown and become much more important. Whereas before record companies had often given teens what they thought they should hear, now teens were making their voices heard—and very loudly. In part, perhaps, it was because music had become so fragmented. There were those who liked alternative, those into dance, or whatever. But the vast majority were still heavily into pop music, they knew what they liked, and they knew what they wanted. And a lot of them wanted the Moffatts.

When the album was finally released in Germany—the first country to get it—anticipation was high, not only from the fans, but also from the record company. Both the singles had done well, and they were expecting great things from the band. They weren't to be disappointed. The records were selling as fast as clerks could ring them up, and within a week *Chapter 1: A New Beginning* had appeared on the charts. The album's title was quite self-explanatory. This *was* a new beginning, and the weeks they'd spent recording at the Gallery Studio in New York had seemed like the first chapter of this part of their lives.

While they were pop musicians now, and stars, they weren't about to deny their past. They were proud of all they'd achieved in country music. If it hadn't been for that, they knew they wouldn't have been where they were now. Every experience fed into a stream, then a river, to bring them to where they were today.

Within a matter of weeks, the Moffatts found themselves with a record that first went gold, and then platinum in Germany. They'd definitely made it to the big time. However, while in America a gold record means sales of half a million, and platinum a million, that sales figure varies from country to country. However, to go gold anywhere you have to sell at least fifty thousand copies, and one hundred thousand for platinum—still not exactly a shabby figure. When they went to the record company to be presented with their gold and platinum records, all framed, it was one of the high points of their lives.

"It's unbelievable getting these platinum albums," Scott said. "We're giving some to our grandparents in Vancouver."

Little could they know that ceremony would be the first of many, all over the globe, and that they'd end up with more platinum records than they knew what to do with, each representing an achievement and a victory for the music they believed in. Things were moving in a whirlwind around them. EMI had already announced that the first single would be released immediately all over Asia and in the boys' homeland of Canada, followed shortly by *Chapter 1: A New Beginning*. In the wake of the success in Germany, excitement was high everywhere. It looked as if the boys were going to be a huge international success. Life was about to get very crazy; it was as if they'd been in first gear, and now they were moving straight into fourth.

Touring Germany and Austria was going to seem like a vacation compared to the schedule that was ahead of them. There was a trip to Asia scheduled, taking in Malaysia, Singapore, the Philippines, and Hong Kong. After that they were headed across the Pacific, to Canada. This wouldn't be a family visit, though, but work, making appearances across the country. Then it would be back to Asia, before heading home to Germany for a short rest. Then there was another German tour, followed by a few days in Britain. That would be enough to fill anyone's summer. And every single day the guys would have home schooling with their dad—not even a summer vacation from that for them among all the other work.

They'd hoped their music would be well received, but they'd never imagined anything on a scale like this. It was just insane. The Philippines, in particular, seemed to love their music; the record had barely appeared before it had gone platinum, and seemed to be glued to the top of the charts. The shows there had been set up before the album's release, and so they found themselves playing in malls that simply couldn't hold the crowds that wanted to see them. They'd also been booked on two lunchtime television shows, where they not only chatted with the host, but also performed, giving them exposure to a much wider audience (as well as letting everyone know that they could really play). During one of their shows, at Manila's SM Megamall, there were so many fans in and around the place, that the Moffatts couldn't even get out of the building.

Like the rest of the world, the Philippines had already had BSB mania and 'N Sync fever, but this was different. These guys didn't just sing. They could whip up the excitement with their own songs or covers (they'd added a Collective Soul tune to their set). And people responded.

But if the Philippines had seemed over the top, that was nothing compared to Malaysia, where the record had taken off even before the boys ever landed in the country. The original shows had been rearranged for larger venues, because of demand, and also for safety reasons. It was probably just as well, given that a mall appearance there brought in a dangerously large audience of *ten thousand* people—more than most bands could ever hope to draw to a concert.

To the guys, this was all shattering. They were constantly on the move, greeted everywhere by armies of fans—it seemed as if the numbers grew with every single appearance, and they probably did. As soon as they showed their faces on stage, the screamers just went wild; they could barely hear themselves play. It was like the Beatles in their heyday.

One thing it didn't make them wonder was why they hadn't turned to pop music before. Quite simply, they hadn't been ready—either as people or as musicians. And when they'd been singing country, it was because they genuinely loved it. There'd been nothing fake in that, just as there was nothing false in this new approach. That had been their music then, this was their music now, and they'd thrown themselves wholeheartedly into both. The reactions they were getting now were way over the top, and there was no way they could have handled anything like that when they were younger.

CHAPTER 8

One of the best things about Asia—apart from picking up more gold and platinum albums, and playing to literally thousands of fans—was that it prepared them for Canada. By the time they landed in Vancouver, able to briefly see their grandparents, *Chapter 1: A New Beginning* had already gone gold. They were stars.

In a way, it wasn't too surprising. There were a lot of bands in Canada, but few who went on to international success. And Canada treasured its bands. MuchMusic, the Canadian MTV, had a policy of featuring Canadian music, and at least twenty percent of the music played by radio stations had to be by Canadian artists. It gave homegrown talent a chance in a marketplace that was increasingly monopolized by big international conglomerates, as the record labels had become. And it helped make stars of a bunch of bands, people like Barenaked Ladies, who might otherwise never have had much of a chance.

A lot of people remembered the Moffatts from when they were younger, since they'd been a fairly well-known attraction then. But these Moffatts, older, much cuter, and playing music to appeal to teens, were something else altogether. All the teen bands with major followings had come from America, even if they'd become big in Canada before they had at home. But Canada had never had a big teen band of its own, and it immediately took the Moffatts to heart. Wherever they played, it was pure insanity.

At Polo Park Mall in Winnipeg, for example, more than two thousand teenage girls packed the place when the Moffatts did a twenty-minute show. Compared to other places they'd played, that might not have seemed a lot, but given that Winnipeg was the only big city in the province of Manitoba, and not really near anywhere else, it was a huge crowd. The mall was so packed with teens that no one could actually shop.

"It was really good, even though you could barely see them," one girl commented. The truth was, you could barely hear them, either, over the screams of the fans. The people who owned stores in the mall were somewhat less enthusiastic about the performance. "This is the worst idea the mall has ever had," one tenant said. "We have no business."

But, ever since Tiffany had made her first appearances in malls a decade before, on a mall tour of the U.S., it had become common practice to hold shows there, particularly shows that would appeal to teens. Since it was one of the places teens congregated, it all made sense—and it brought business into the mall. Before and after the shows, the teens would shop.

Well, maybe not before every show. In Winnipeg, fans of the Moffats had begun arriving as early as five-thirty A.M. for a show that didn't start until two P.M.. By the time the mall opened at ten, there were already more than five hundred kids gathered and ready, staking out their places to be able to see the boys. Once they hit the stage—escorted there by security guards—they were showered with flowers, stuffed animals, love notes, and even phone numbers written on scraps of paper.

It was a short set, just time to run through their major songs, plus a cover by one of their major influences, the Beatles' "She Loves You," before leaving. But it wasn't all over yet. Every place they played in Canada was special to the guys. Becoming stars in other parts of the globe was cool, but the adulation at home was something pretty amazing. So they hung around in a special roped-off area, metting and greeting, and happily signing autographs for two hours before they finally had to be dragged away to their next commitment.

Certainly, the fans couldn't have been happier with all the attention they received, and for the guys themselves, it was a great opportunity for them to meet some Canadian girls. The last time they'd toured the country, they were young, and hadn't cared about the opposite sex. But things had changed, and they'd grown up a lot.

"The women are great all over Canada," Scott says. "They're just good-looking, really nice."

"We always appreciated them," Bob adds.

"But we've taken in a lot more now," Scott laughs.

What happened in Winnipeg was just typical of scenes throughout the country. Wherever the band played, they drew massive crowds. At the Wonderland amusement park (another natural venue), they pulled in almost ten thousand fans, all eager to hear and see their homeboys. Nothing could have made them happier than to receive all this praise and friendship in their own country. It made coming home again very wonderful.

Eventually, though, it was time to leave Canada and head back to Asia, for their second tour there in three months. People simply wanted to see them. Their album was still selling like the proverbial hotcakes, they were drawing massive crowds wherever they played, especially in the Philippines, Malaysia, and Singapore. All three places seemed to have fallen in love with them.

It made perfect sense to tour there when they were hot, but there was something else that had to be considered. There were other important markets they hadn't touched yet, primarily Britain. That one was going to be tough. Boy bands (and girls bands, for that matter) had always done well there, and Britons loved pop music. But it was the homegrown talent that generally made it, not imports from America, or, in this case, Canada. Even Hanson hadn't really made much of an impression there. Could the Moffatts be the ones to break the jinx?

They'd find out soon enough. And a trip to Great Britain would also give the family a chance to investigate their roots a little. They knew the family name was Scottish, and that there was a small town called Moffatt there. It was part of their plans, while there, to take a few days and find this place, to see where some ancestor of theirs had started his journey west.

The boys all loved London. Compared to many of the countries they'd seen, it seemed *so* hip and fashionable. Scott in particular—the brother who'd first got into fashion—was amazed, according to Clint. "He saw the fashion over there and he just loved it." Certainly it seemed way ahead of Canada or America, and the guys, especially Scott, found themselves spending quite a bit on clothes. But that was fine; after all, they had to look good on stage.

This was one of the few countries where the single had been released, but hadn't charted. The album had just come out, and had received a little airplay. The guys appeared on a few radio shows, did some television, and a couple of concerts, but still *Chapter 1: A New Beginning* didn't seem to be taking off. It was frustrating. Not because they expected to do well everywhere, but because Britain was a place they respected, as a country and musically, and they felt it was particularly important to make their make there.

However, that wasn't going to happen immediately, by the look of things. So they decided to forget about it, relax, and enjoy their brief Scottish vacation.

Finding the village of Moffatt—and it was definitely more of a village than a town—wasn't easy. It was in Dumfries and Galloway County, not far from Edinburgh, and close to the Firth of Forth. Once, a long time ago, it had been far out in the country. Now, as the cities had grown, it had become an extended part of suburbia. But it was still quiet there, so quiet, in fact, that when Clint asked a local if there was anything worth seeing in the area, the reply was, "Anytime you come to Moffatt, just keep driving."

Boys will be boys . . . with Mom and Dad.
(© BETH GWINN/RETNA)

Back when they were working on the songs that made them famous. (© BETH GWINN/RETNA)

Scott, Dave, Clint, Bob, and Frank Moffatt.
(© BETH GWINN/RETNA)

All grown up and looking good . . .
(© John Gladwin/Retna)

Say cheese . . .
(© John Gladwin/Retna)

Scott and Clint rip it up onstage.
(© NICKY J. SIMS/SOUND REPUBLIC/REDFERNS/RETNA)

Scott putting the song across.
(© Nicky J. Sims/Sound Republic/Redferns/Retna)

Boys will be men.
(© JOHN GLADWIN/ALL ACTION/RETNA)

While it didn't seem as bad as *that* to the brothers, it wasn't quite the romantic place they'd always had in their heads. Even Frank, older and more used to life's disappointments, was sad.

All in all, their visit to Britain hadn't been the best thing that had ever happened to them, although Bob managed to fall in love with London.

"It's definitely a happening city," he says. "The people are very nice and their accents are very cool." A shame, then, that the English didn't warm to the Moffatts.

By now they'd literally been around the world, and it was back to Germany to chill out and decompress for a little while. And after that? Well, they had to go back and do it all over again, of course. Lots of places were still mad for them, in particular Asia, where Thailand had joined the countries coming down with Moffatts fever.

One downside to being on the road so much was that it made it difficult to have relationships. Both Scott and Bob had had girlfriends in the past. Bob's had been called Maria, and, ironically, she'd moved from America to Canada. Scott's former girlfriend, back in Nashville, was named Angie. Both Bob and Scott remained friends with their exes, but all four of the brothers (Dave had actually *never* had a girlfriend) were now very much single. Given the way girls were hurling themselves at them, that might not have been a bad thing. But these days they were never in one place long enough to get to know anyone.

And sometimes the reactions from female fans could be quite puzzling. One time, in Spain, a girl managed to evade security and sneak into their hotel room. The boys were dressed—just—in their boxers.

"She started *crying*," Clint recalls.

"If we walked into a room with Pamela Anderson in the same clothes, we would *not* be crying!" Scott laughed.

So relationships were out of the question for the moment, but they all understood and reluctantly accepted that. Music and the family had been their focus for so long that it was second nature to them now. And both were still hugely, majorly important to all four of them. They knew each other much better than most brothers ever would, and they knew far more about the world—and had seen more of the world—than the vast majority of teenagers. The fact that they'd become stars almost overnight (and it seemed that way to them, too, even with all the years of groundwork they'd put in) was icing on the cake. Simply being able to play music for people and be paid for it was reward enough for them. It made them ridiculously happy.

After a week in Germany, looking at fan mail, doing laundry, and just beginning to remember what a normal life was like, it was time to hit the road again, playing a few concerts around Europe, before heading back to the Far East for the third time in less than a year.

By now they had their stage show down to an exact science. One thing they loved to do was to involve the audience, getting them to clap on the beat to some songs, and for a sing-along section, dividing the audience into two halves, and seeing "which half could scream the loudest."

At the same time, they'd really developed as a band. They could take a song like "Wild at Heart" and turn it into something of a jam, giving both Scott and Clint a chance to shine as they exchanged riffs—something the audience always loved.

They weren't above teasing the audience a bit, either, and both playing up to and making fun of the heartthrob image they'd acquired. At almost every show, Scott would slowly remove his sweat-soaked T-shirt, then pour most of a bottle of water over his chest, before spraying the rest over the front rows. It was an act that always drew a lot of screams.

This tour took them into the Philippines (three times!), Singapore, Malaysia, Hong Kong, and Thailand. The Philippine tour was actually in three legs, and would bring them close to Christmas. By now they could have contented themselves playing major venues, but there was more to them than that. The Philippines had been early supporter of the band, and they wanted to show their thanks. So there were autograph sessions at a record store (Ratsky's in Greenhills), and even a concert in a school gym, at Sacred Heart School for Boys in Cebu City.

Not that they didn't play the big venues, too. It all climaxed with a massive show at the Big Dome in Manila, which drew literally thousands of fans. And the boys did it up big style, starting out with "I'll Be There for You" and never letting up the excitement through a set that lasted over an hour, finishing with "Santa Claus is Coming to Town," their version based on the Bruce Springsteen cover of the Christmas classic. Along the way they played their new single, which was already high on the charts, "Girl of My Dreams," which Clint dedicated to all the girls who'd come to see them. They even delved way, way back to do a song they'd done on the Christmas cassette they'd released in 1995, when they were still a country band, slowing down the pace for a few minutes with an acoustic rendition of "How Would Jesus Feel?" a reminder of the real meaning of the holiday season.

It was one of the best shows they'd ever played, the atmosphere totally electric even before they appeared, and that made it the perfect way to round out the year before flying back to Germany. There was time to relax and recharge their batteries, because they were going to need every ounce of energy. The new year was just around the corner, and there were huge plans for 1999. If '98 had seemed incredible, well, the best was yet to come. . . .

CHAPTER 9

What was so magical about *Chapter 1: A New Beginning* that it drove people wild in so many countries? Produced by David Brunner and the Berman Brothers, it had been recorded, for the most part, at Gallery Studios in New York, with almost all the remaining tracks completed at Metalworks Studios, in Mississauga, Ontario, Canada. The only exception was "Love," which the Moffatts had written and recorded in Germany, at Dierks Studio, where they had done all their rehearsing. And that track also marked the brothers' production debut, on a song co-written by Scott and Greg Rowles. "Say'n I Love U" was another song written by all four of the brothers, while Frank had joined them in composing "Girl of My Dreams," and Sheila helped her stepsons with "If Life is So Short." The other songs came from the pens of the Berman Brothers, Dave Brunner, and Jeff Coplan, with help here and there from D. Metreyeon.

Coplan had also helped fill out the instrumental sound on the album (the horns on "Say'n I Love U" were by David Mann and Berry Danielian). Otherwise, as was pointed out in the liner notes, all the instruments had been played by the Moffatts themselves—and one thing they made sure of was the inclusion of some fake graffiti in among the song lyrics, pointing out "No Drugs" and "No Cigarettes."

While the American version of the record would offer some more tracks, from the pen and production talents of Glen Ballard, it was the thirteen tracks the rest of the world heard on *Chapter 1: A New Beginning* that made the Moffatts as hot as a four-alarm blaze.

It all began with "Wild at Heart," which used a chord sequence and guitar sound very similar to Nirvana's "Smells Like Teen Spirit" (and also the old Monkees' song, ("I'm Not Your Stepping Stone"), just exploding out of the speakers on the chords before Scott launched into the first verse. Once it got going, of course, it was nothing like the Nirvana tune. Instead it was much poppier and accessible, not about alienation (as so much of Kurt Cobain's material had been), but about being, well... wild. You could think of it as a manifesto for the new Moffatts, and the way they were going to be from now on. While they might not have been exactly wild themselves, there was no doubt this was something new for the band, the perfect summation of the pop rock sound they'd been experimenting with for several months, and a strong indication of how well they'd learned to play their instruments. It was easy to see how it would quickly become a concert favorite, with its strong riff, and possibilities for jamming at the end.

"Miss You Like Crazy" was a complete contrast, slower, softer, based around an acoustic guitar and Bob's percussion, with the harmonies they'd developed in full effect, especially on the chorus. Dave's keyboard sounded like a string section to punctuate between verses. It was a lovely song, very romantic and full in its sound, changing key to bring out Scott's guitar solo, before finishing off with the repeated chorus and those sweet voices working so beautifully and naturally together.

It was the guys themselves who'd written "Say'n I Love U" and they seemed to bring a special energy to playing it. It started slow, like a soul ballad, with horns over the top, before going into a ska beat, obviously influenced by bands like the Mighty Mighty Bosstones, Reel Big Fish, and No Doubt, particularly in the way the words of the lyrics crossed over lines. It was totally infectious. Interestingly, the chord progression was reminiscent of the Beatles' "She Loves You," a song the Moffatts sometimes covered at their shows. There was no denying that it was a very cool tune, and lyrically wise—he might be slow to say he loved her, but when he did, it would be for real, no playing around. Scott got to take the solo—and he was a skilled guitar player. The bridge slowed things down a little, then hanging time before kicking back in, picking back up on the chorus. It was the type of thing to get all the suits skanking on the dance floor.

"Girl of My Dreams," another tune from the boys, along with Frank, seemed to set the pace of the album at uptempo song followed by ballad. Again, it was the harmonies over the acoustic guitar, with bass and drums in the background, Dave's keyboard making a wash of chords on which it could all rest. It was a plea to a girl he'd treated badly, and whom now wished he'd treated better, realizing just how much he missed her. Again, it was Scott who took the solo—his guitar really did seem to be the band's lead instrument. The song's chorus just took up residence in your mind and refused to leave; it was impossible not to hum along with it.

"Crazy" was pure rock 'n' roll, distorted guitar chords leading the way. If not for the sweetness of Scott's voice, it was the type of thing that could easily have been played, and very successfully, on a modern rock station. But it was the chorus that was the real killer, once the backing vocals and their oh-oh-oh-oh-ohs came in. The beat just drove along relentlessly, and this song truly established their credentials to be taken seriously as a bunch of rockers. Scott's guitar just went berserk near the end, and the effects were quite spacey, before the chorus yanked you back in. Even someone who didn't like rock—and if anyone was going to make rock cool again, it was the Moffatts—would have been forced to admit it was a great song.

"Don't Walk Away" wasn't strictly a ballad, more midtempo, underpinned by Scott's acoustic guitar chords, and giving the guys plenty of opportunity to hit those brotherly harmonies on the chorus, while Scott sang the verses, as usual. Back in the Eighties, the arrangement would have layered on the electric guitars in the chorus, for what was called a "power ballad." This was more subtle, however, even down to the key change, which added some variety, finishing gently with just the guitar. It was a good song, just not a standout on a record that had so many brilliant performances.

The next song, "Now and Forever," definitely hit Nineties territory with a percussion loop running behind the vocals, including a chorus that could almost have been pulled from a Seventies bubblegum tune. Again, it was midtempo, with Scott's acoustic very much in evidence. The highlight here was the voices, with harmonies that mere friends could never achieve, and a sing-along section at the end that would translate wonderfully into a concert performance.

"Love" was very special to the boys, given that they not only wrote it, but were also responsible for the production (the first time they'd done that), undertaken in Germany when they were living there—which made it a late addition to the album. Still, it was a very worthwhile addition. Scott had a chance to do some lovely picking on a gorgeous ballad. The multi-tracked guitars took the first verse, then bass and congas backed him on the second, with quiet little touches from Dave's keyboards weaving around it all on the second chorus. Mostly, though, it was a vehicle for some heartfelt lyrics that were all about (surprise!) ... love. In some of the vocal arrangement you could hear the Moffatts' past in country—and with a slightly different slant, this could easily have been a massive country hit.

The song that had first made the Moffatts into international stars was "I'll Be There for You," and that was next up. It started with a funky little guitar line, over a cowbell, the kind of thing to get you bouncing in your seat. Then the voices kicked in, and it became more infectious than the chickenpox. It was pure pop for now people, the kind of thing you only needed to hear once to have it permanently lodged in your brain, totally impossible to resist. The na-na refrain behind it all was little short of wonderful. The chorus was great, and there were enough little elements going on in the song—the electric guitar over the acoustic, and the different rhythms working together—to keep it all really intriguing. At the same time there was a straightforward beat, and super-powerful vocals, especially on the chorus. It was easy to see how it became such a huge hit in so many places around the world. This was the sound of a band who really had their act together, who obviously were totally in love with pop music, and loved the kick of rock 'n' roll.

The only thing that could follow that was a pure ballad, and that's exactly what "Girl I'm Gonna Get You" was. Dave's piano was to the fore during the verses, over Scott's guitar arpeggios and Bob's congas. The chorus had quite a sweep (courtesy of Dave's synthesizer), and it seemed something of a gesture to the big BSB-type ballads, with those exact, fraternal harmonies. Scott once again proved how good and tasteful a guitarist he was when he had the chance to solo—it wasn't how fast he played, but *what* he chose to play that made him so good. It was a song that had hit written all over it, if it was released as a single.

Then it was time to heat things back up with "We Are Young." It wasn't a hard rocker, with Scott's acoustic guitar in evidence, more an out-and-out pop song that played up the harmonies. And why not? They were so perfect they deserved to be heard often and loudly, so close that they could almost sound like one voice, which in some ways they were, connected by blood. Scott's electric solo blew the song out of the water, building the excitement that exploded when the boys sang the chorus without accompaniment as they came back in. It was a killer, another one of so many on this record.

The guys had written "If Life is so Short" with their stepmother, Sheila, something of a first for them, and it was a song that seemed to begin like a ballad, before the chorus took off at mid-pace. Again, it was those wonderful harmonies that caught the ear, but it was also apparent that they had a great ear for a catchy chorus, and also a hook, something to draw the listener in and make them want to keep listening. And, once more, Scott showed himself to be an inventive, thoughtful guitar player, the type any band would be happy to have as a member. All that, and he could sing and he was cute, too! But they all were....

Again it was one of those give me another chance songs, but since relationships do break up and get back together, there was absolutely nothing wrong with that. It stood in great contrast to the album's final track, "Jump," which was just about moving, dancing, and enjoying life. This had a funky wah-wah opening, but it didn't explode into the high-energy outing people probably expected. Instead it was a bit more restrained, but built during the verse, leading into a strong chorus. The rhythm owed a bit to dance music, but that was fine—this is the late Nineties, after all. But one thing you weren't going to find in a Moffatts song was hip-hop; that wasn't what they were about.

Those were all the tracks listed on the sleeve, but if you carried on listening, after another thirty seconds you hit the "hidden" track, called "Frustration," which was just Scott solo with his acoustic guitar. And it was something very different, much more personal, something that seemed to owe more to alternative music than pop—but still good. From the quality and roughness of the playing, it sounded like a demo he'd recorded, possibly for the band to work out, but it ended up standing as it was. It was a song of several parts, ending the way it had begun, quietly, and very moving.

At just over fifty minutes (including that hidden track) it certainly wasn't the longest album ever released. But it was quality, rather than quantity, that was always the issue with a record. Sure, you could get over seventy-five minutes on a CD, but if no one wanted to hear it, what was the point? Virtually every track on *Chapter 1: A New Be-*

ginning could have stood as a single, and a successful one at that.

Certainly the album was successful. In Canada it ended up platinum, in Indonesia double platinum, with the same in Malaysia. Thailand turned it triple platinum, while in the Philippines—which had been mad for the boys—it went five times platinum. Spain, Portugal, and Singapore all brought forward gold records for the boys. It was amazing.

In fact, in Asia, when they toured there, the band had put out a special album called *P.S. I Love You*, which, with the same tracks, was called *Tour Souvenir Package* in the Philippines. It contained "Miss You Like Crazy," "Crazy," "I'll Be There for You," "Girl of My Dreams," "If Life is So Short," "Ya Ya," "Girls of the World," "Lara My Love," "If Life is So Short (Live)," and "Say'n I Love U (Live)." Obviously, quite a few of those tracks weren't on *Chapter 1: A New Beginning*, but they had appeared in various parts of the world as extra tracks on singles, along with a couple of others.

The European single of "Girl of My Dreams," for example, as well as containing a live version of the song, and a remix of "Crazy," also contained "Over the Rainbow (Garage Recording)." It was a song the brothers had written and produced themselves, and it was, as it says, a rough recording, without too much studio polish. It wouldn't have had a place on the album, being *too* alternative. It was based around a riff from Dave's synth and Clint's bass, with Scott thrashing chords over the top. It sounded as though it had been recorded live. The harmonies weren't sweet, and it wasn't the best thing they'd ever written, but it gave them an outlet for that side of their personalities—the same vague teen isolation that had been evident on "Frustration."

The U.K. version of "Crazy" had two tracks that weren't on the album, "Ya Ya" and "Lara My Love." "Ya Ya," written by the boys with Frank and Sheila, had been recorded at Dierks Studio while they were in Germany. The main instrument was Scott's acoustic guitar, strumming fast, while all the brothers sang, really highlighting the harmonies that were one of their trademarks. It was one of those philosophical songs that made you think about the meaning of life, with a catchy chorus. Even so, it would have sounded too spare on the album, although it was a very strong song, somewhat reminiscent of the late Sixties or early Seventies in style, a kind of folk-rock.

"Lara My Love" also featured Scott's acoustic picking, and came close to singer-songwriter territory, very romantic—you had to wonder who it had been written for. It was composed by the family, along with Hagen Breide and Klaus "Major" Heuser. It was gentle, with Bob's congas soft in the background, Dave's keyboard sketching the melody between verses, and Clint's bass keeping time. It was something guaranteed to keep fans happy during the acoustic portion of a Moffatts show.

All these songs served notice that the band wasn't about to let themselves be limited or straitjacketed by any musical form. They were still young, very eager, and taking in everything. They liked too many musical styles to just stick with one, and they were developing, as musicians and songwriters, at a very rapid rate. More than anything, it raised the question of where they'd be in a couple of years—they were pushing ahead at the speed of sound.

But by the time Capitol Records was ready to release *Chapter 1: A New Beginning* in America, there was nothing brand-new on the album. The boys had been playing the songs for over a year. Something fresh was needed, some infusion of new blood. New tracks were an option, and the label wanted to team the band with a producer and writer who seemed to have his finger on the commercial pulse of America, rather than Europe or Asia (the aim, after all, was to break them through to the other side in the U.S.). The obvious choice was Glen Ballard. His work with Alanis Morrissette on *Jagged Little Pill* had helped make that album, and Morrissette, into something envied throughout the record industry, and he'd also worked with Michael Jackson and Aerosmith, which pretty much covered the whole gamut of music. What the man touched seemed to turn to gold (or platinum).

And so Capitol put the Moffatts in the studio with Ballard, to see what would happen. The result was four new songs—"Until You Loved Me," "Written All Over My Heart," "Misery," and "Raining in My Mind," the last co-written by the boys with Ballard, who produced all the tracks, giving them a slightly fuller sound than they'd had before.

Not surprisingly, the band sounded a little wiser, a little more developed on these cuts. They'd been playing their own particular brand of music for quite a while now, they'd tightened it up and had new ideas, helped by Ballard, who wasn't afraid to try something slightly different (he played the sitar on "Until You Loved Me" and encouraged Scott to use the mandolin on the introduction to "Misery"), while still retaining the same general sound that highlighted the boys' music.

"You need to expand to the next level," Dave says. "You have to grow with the fans and grow with the music." And that was exactly what they'd done. Working with Ballard had been an inspiring time, and it turned out to be one he'd loved, too.

"It was unequivocally a positive experience," he says. "They are very gifted musicians. I was impressed with their focus, their discipline, the way they played together as a unit." While the Moffatts prided themselves on being easy to work with, getting such praise made them feel very good indeed. They'd been approved by one of the hottest guys in the business.

There was a careful strategy to help them in America. It was, after all, the biggest market in the world for music, and that meant it was the most difficult to break into. Obviously, it would have been easiest to simply release the record and hope for the best, trusting that people would find it and that it would get radio airplay. But that wasn't the best way for the band to reach an audience, especially the audience they wanted. There was already a major buzz from all over the world, but at the beginning of 1999 how many Americans had ever heard of the Moffatts? Very few.

It was better to work gradually, and to help that happen, the label got one of the songs the band had done with Glen Ballard on the soundtrack of a movie aimed at teens. It was a perfect mix, really. The movie would bring in the age group who'd love the band, they'd hear the song, see the name, and be primed. *Never Been Kissed* starred Drew Barrymore in a sweet comedy—completing her image change from the wild child she'd been a few years before—with plenty of cool music playing, mostly new, but also including older tracks by the Smiths ("Please, Please, Please, Let Me Get What I Want"), John Lennon and Yoko Ono ("Watching the Wheels"), and the Beach Boys ("Don't Worry Baby"). The new bands were Semisonic, Willis, Jimmy Eat World, Remy Zero, the Cardigans, Kendall Payne, R.E.M., Block, Swirl 360, Ozomati, Sonichrome, and Jeremy Jordan.

Given the romantic element of the film, the natural Moffatts' song was "Until You Loved Me." It showed both their rock and pop sides, and stood out in a soundtrack that was full of highlights. And not surprisingly, it was also planned as the boys' first single. While the movie had appeared in March, the single wouldn't actually appear until the end of April, giving audiences a chance to become familiar with the name of the Moffatts. Quite cleverly, the single also contained snippets of three of the tracks from the album—"Misery," "Written All Over My Heart" (both songs produced by Glen Ballard), along with "Miss You Like Crazy." There was also the non-album track, "Let's Party," which had previously appeared in Asia. It was a nice acoustic romp, written by the boys along with Sheila and Frank, showing another side of their personalities, and highlighting the harmonies in a simple frame.

The April release would give the Moffatts a chance to tour and promote the single, as well as give Americans their first taste of *Chapter 1: A New Beginning*, the expanded version of which was set to hit the U.S. stores in June.

During March and the first half of April, the boys would be touring extensively in Canada, consolidating their success and hopefully building on it. The album had gone platinum, but double platinum was just down the road. They even found time, on April 20, to play an all-ages show at a club in New York City. Playing for all ages was very important to them. Not only were the majority of their fans under twenty-one, but they were, too; they knew what it was like not to be able to go and see their favorite bands.

In fact, from April 26, when "Until You Loved Me" was released as a single in America, the boys' schedule would be increasingly hectic. From the twenty-sixth to the end of the month there would be a whirlwind cross-country promotional tour, speaking to radio disc jockeys, press, and everyone, culminating in an appearance on May 1 at the Nickelodeon Kids' Choice Awards.

From there it was straight off to England, where they'd be busy with promotion and shows until the sixteenth, including two major concerts, one on the ninth at Manchester Debating Hall, and an even bigger one to finish their time there, at London's Shepherd's Bush Empire on the sixteenth.

All that would be followed by a well-earned vacation until the twenty-eighth of May, giving them a chance to wind down and catch up on their sleep. Soon enough, however, they'd be back at it again. From June 3 to the twenty-sixth there'd be a U.S. tour, both concerts and promotion. No sooner was that complete, than they'd head north of the border, touring and promoting in Canada until mid-July, after which it was back on the American concert and promotional trail until the end of July.

By then, beyond any doubt, they'd be exhausted, so the first couple of weeks of August had been set aside for vacation. On the thirteenth they'd resume work with a concert close to home, in Manchester, Tennessee, at Itchycoo Park, a place named after an old Small Faces song. Then, for the next ten days, they'd be crisscrossing America again, before heading back to Canada until the twenty-eighth. From August 29 until September 8, there were more U.S. dates, after which they'd hop on a plane and travel to the U.K., where they'd stay on the road until the twenty-first. And was there another vacation? Not a chance. From England it was directly on to Asia, their first time there in 1999, to tour from September 22 until October 12. Then, finally, they'd drop and sleep—for a little while, anyway.

It was a truly shattering schedule, so it was just as well that they loved what they were doing. And also that they were young and resilient, able to cope with all the travel and lack of sleep involved in touring. Coming off stage, their adrenalin would be soaring near the stratosphere, meaning there'd be no sleep for a few hours. Just about the time they'd be getting comfortable in bed, it would be time to get up and get on an airplane or bus again. But they believed in themselves, and their music, and that kept them going, always eager to perform for fans old and new. And they knew how lucky they were. How many kids their age got to travel all over the world and play music for a living? At sixteen and fifteen, most kids were having a hard time even putting a band together, if they played at all.

Of course, they'd spent a number of years paying their dues, and learning the business from the inside out. But all that knowledge had paid off big time. It might still have been hard to take in, but the fact was that in a lot of places around the globe they were major stars. They drew huge crowds of fans.

In some ways, it was as if they all had two completely separate lives. They were the Moffatts, with records out, and lots of girls screaming at them wherever they went. But they were also Scott, Dave, Clint, and Bob, four regular guys who were still being home-schooled by their father, and who enjoyed the regular things in life when they had a break from the road or the studio.

Having moved back to Nashville, having that ordinary life became a bit easier. For all of them, their German had improved while living in Pulheim-Strommeln, but it was still good to be "home." Living abroad had been an adventure (and a risk, really—there was never any guarantee they'd hit it really big in Germany, let alone other parts of the world), but now they were ready to concentrate on America and add that to their list of conquests. To be fair, they also wanted to win over Britain, but America was the real focus. If they made it there, then they'd really succeeded. In Tennessee they could catch up with their old friends, see their mother regularly, and really be a family again, able to go out and do things when they had time off. Even if it was just playing basketball—which was something they'd have the chance to do on television. In April, they'd taped an episode of the Saturday morning show, *Hang Time*, which featured them, among other things, shooting some hoops. They might not be candidates for the N.B.A. anytime soon, but they had fun—and that, after all, was the whole point of life. Sure, it helped promote the album, and would probably air in May or in June—when *Chapter 1: A New Beginning* would hit the record stores all across America—but it was more than that. It was something that gave them the chance to show something of themselves, the guys behind the stage persona.

Obviously, there was a lot at stake in America. It was the biggest market in the world for music. But everyone believed they could make it there. They had the experience and the enthusiasm.

"We've been singing for eleven years now and it just keeps on getting more exciting all the time," Scott says, adding, "We knew when we were four that we wanted to make music, and in fifty years' time we still will."

It's that type of dedication to the music, regardless of the success, that will help them to become massive stars in America, and in Britain, giving them a real global pop domination. As Bob says, "We'll be coming to your town soon! We can't wait to meet you!"

They know how to put on an amazing show, and how to entertain an audience. But after doing that professionally for seven years, that's only to be expected. They use the stage well, and Scott in particular likes to move around, especially when he's taking a solo (well, it is kind of hard for Bob and Dave to move around too much, when they're behind the drums and keyboards). They can heat it up, getting wilder and wilder, then cool it down again with some acoustic ballads. In short, they've got it all going on, from the voices to the rock 'n' roll. While they've become used to playing big arenas in other parts of the world, they know that America will have to be won over, and that's going to mean a lot of smaller shows, a lot of meeting people, and talking on the radio.

But everything will be done with a smile. Apart from the fact that they're polite, and some of the most agreeable people you could hope to meet, this is it for them. This is their opportunity to become massive, and they'd play every home in America if it would help them. Of course, they won't have to be that extreme. America will love them, just the way other countries have. The charts already prove that teens are hungry for good pop music, in all its forms, and the Moffatts make some of the best. With a band, the guitar never goes out of style, and in Scott, the band has a guitar star.

It's still going to be a long haul, a lot of shows and appearances, and a lot of traveling. But it's all going to work out just fine. America will wonder how it ever lived without Moffatt music, and there'll be Moffatt mania throughout the land.

And who knows—maybe there'll be a double bill somewhere of the Moffatts and Hanson, which would be a very cool show. And it could be even more fun before the fans started arriving.

"We wouldn't mind getting together and jamming with them sometime in a rehearsal hall," Bob says. "That would be pretty cool, a couple of young bands just getting their instruments on and jamming together."

It's food for thought, and probably a wish for millions, if only to be a fly on the wall when and if that ever happened. And anything's possible. . . .

PART THREE
THE BOYS

Scott

It's hardly a state secret that Scott Andrew Moffatt is the oldest of the brothers, born not quite twelve months before the others, on March 30, 1983. He's also the only one not to be born in British Columbia, instead starting his life in Whitehorse, in the Canadian Yukon. Considering he was there less than a year, however, for all intents and purposes he might as well have been born in B.C.—it was certainly the place where he grew up with the others.

As the guitarist, frontman, and in some ways the leader of the band (although the others might disagree with him on that part!), Scott has a lot of responsibility. He's the one who takes the solos, so he has to be the best musician, and on the ballads, it's his guitar that provides the instrumental cushion for all the harmonies. That's a lot of weight to carry in the studio, and even more live—but he's up to it.

At sixteen, he seems to have largely found himself. Certainly he's discovered what he wants to do with the rest of his life—which is more than most people his age can say. But then again, it's eleven years since he first performed; if he didn't enjoy music, he'd have probably found out by now.

While all the traveling of the last couple of years has made him something of a citizen of the world, home still remains North America, and he's certainly not going to deny his Canadian side (his favorite actress is a Canadian,

Neve Campbell of *Party of Five*). The boys' grandparents still live in Vancouver, and the brothers go there when the chance arises—which isn't as often as they might like these days—they're simply *too* busy.

With the relative freedom of being in the music business (and no school dress code since they're all schooled at home), Scott's been able to let his hair grow. It's still growing, too. The cover picture for the version of *Chapter 1: A New Beginning* that was released elsewhere in the world shows him with hair to the base of his neck. Now, more than a year later, it flows onto his shoulders, not as full as before. But the blond streak at the front? That's been there for a little while. And the last year has seen the last vestiges of the baby fat leave his face. He's gone from looking like a boy to looking like a man. A very hunky man, at that.

He might be the oldest, but given the relative closeness in ages, it doesn't often seem that way.

"The funny thing is, I don't feel like the older brother," he explains, "I just think of myself as a brother. It feels like we're the same age."

And in some ways, they're all treated very much the same. All of them have just finished ninth grade, although Scott should really have been a year ahead. But for teaching purposes—given that they're all taught together by their father Frank, whether at home or on the road—this was just easier, allowing them to all study the same subjects together. Of the four, Scott's the standout in social studies.

It should probably come as no surprise that Scott's favorite band is Nirvana, and his all-time favorite song is their massive hit, "Smells Like Teen Spirit." The influence of Kurt Cobain is there in the aggressive way he can play his guitar, and more especially in the way he writes some songs—"Frustration," the hidden extra track at the end of *Chapter 1: A New Beginning* being a prime example. While just an acoustic demo, it was obviously written for a band, with some of the unusual chord changes that Cobain seemed to love employed. And there's also that sense of alienation in the lyrics, which is also true of the rough recording of "Over the Rainbow" the boys added in to a single. Could Scott lead the guys toward alternative music? It's possible, although maybe not. He could, though, develop a solo career, to parallel the Moffatts, doing something like that.

Given his musical tastes, it's perhaps odd to discover that his favorite guitarist is Eric Clapton. More than thirty years ago, Clapton was hailed as the best British guitarist ever, first for his blues playing, and then for his more progressive outlook with bands like Cream, Blind Faith, and Derek and the Dominos. Soon, though, he seemed to veer to the middle of the road, and has stayed quite firmly there ever since, concentrating more on songs than any real virtuosity in his playing. Quite why Scott should single him out, unless he's heard some of those old records, is an interesting question.

However, he might well have heard Clapton's earlier work, since Scott has delved way back, musically. Thanks in part to their father, the boys have all been exposed to a lot of music from the Sixties and Seventies. That's how the Beatles came to have such an influence on their writing style, and probably why Scott names the Beatles' *Abbey Road* as his favorite album. Certainly it was the most complex thing the Fab Four ever did, released right as they split up in 1970. There's a lot of melody in the songs, something the Moffatts rightly pride themselves on having. While the brothers might not be as developed as writers as Lennon and McCartney, they've started from the right basis, studying people who are acknowledged as the greatest pop composers ever—and it's also a sign that the legacy of the Beatles shows no sign of fading. Scott's love of melody is apparent from the fact that his favorite song on the album is "If Life is So Short," which might just showcase the harmonies to greatest effect.

Elvis, as the others nicknamed him for his showbiz style, might be obsessed with music, but that doesn't mean he's not interested in other things. Fashion is a biggie with him, and has been for a few years now.

"I was about twelve when I said I'm going to wear fashionable instead of just whatever I find." Now, of course, he can go shopping for clothes all over the world—assuming he can find the time, that is.

It's a big change from the way the guys all dressed when they were younger. Back then, their father dressed them all identically, making it easier to spot them in crowds. And so there'd be four boys in cowboy hats, shirts, and shorts. But not just regular shirts and shorts. There would be weird combinations like green shorts and pink shirts. Those would certainly stand out in any crowd! But in those days, as the boys *all* point out, they didn't care about girls, so the way they looked wasn't important. Now, for each of them, appearance really matters.

Maybe it's because he's not a triplet, but the others tend to pick on Scott, even though he's older. Maybe that's inevitable, since they share a very special kind of bond that he never can, even if he is family. But, he says, "I don't mind it. I accept it."

As they've grown, each of the boys has developed a very separate personality, with Scott quite definitely the most individual, possibly because he's slightly older. He's the real reader of the group, one who always seems to have a book with him wherever he's traveling. Given some free time: "I will be relaxing. Or playing sports like soccer, American football, and hockey. Or just watching TV, playing my guitar." Obviously, he can't leave music behind for more than a few moments. Still, it's that dedication that's helped to make him such a good player.

And from his interests, it apparent that he's no couch potato. To keep fit on the road, he does "push-ups and sit-ups" in his hotel room—although don't ever expect to find him in line for a bungee jump; the idea terrifies him. He actually did it once, in Nashville, when all the brothers dared each other to try. And for Scott there won't be any next time, that's for sure!

But it's music, though, that fills most of his waking moments. He'd like the Moffatts to be as big as the Beatles once were—and that would be pretty massive. Music is such a big part of his life that on those nights he can't sleep, he finds himself thinking about song ideas. Music, too, has provided the single most embarrassing moment of his life. The Moffatts were playing a big show in Germany, and Scott was running around the stage, as usual. "I fell ... on the stage in front of eight thousand people," he recalls. But being a true professional, he picked himself up and carried on as if nothing had happened—although you can bet that his brothers wouldn't let him forget about it!

If Scott has a fault (and plenty of girls might well say he's perfect), it's his impatience. Having decided on doing something, he wants to do it *now*—whatever it might be. He doesn't wait very well. But, when you get down to it, how many people do? And, like so many others, Scott has a great weakness for chocolate—his only failing, really, since he doesn't drink, doesn't smoke, and definitely doesn't do drugs—which is true for all four of the boys. He does also bite his nails, and likes to chew gum, but that's about as bad as he gets.

Well, maybe he does have one other weakness—girls. It doesn't matter where they're from, he likes them all, although he does seem especially fond of girls from France (that's apart from his native Canada). But he's totally in love with Paris.

"I mean, the atmosphere is perfect," he says. "The girls, the food, everything is just everything I've ever dreamed." He knows from experience, of course, having been there several times, and it remains his favorite vacation destination. Not that he's had a chance to spend any time there alone—yet. But he will when he's a bit older.

And if he does get the chance to go out on a date (and while he's very single now, he was involved with a girl named Angie for a while, but these days they're simply friends), his ideal evening would be "definitely a candlelight dinner. Yeah, definitely a scary movie, then some cozy café for dessert, and then go home." Which wouldn't be a bad way to spend an evening—and a scary movie would give a girl plenty of chances to hold on to her escort.

Quite obviously, family is very important in Scott's life. Given the amount of time he spends around them (something in the range of twenty-four hours a day), that's not too surprising. But none of the brothers really fight, making them one of the most functional families on the planet, and they truly enjoy playing together, whether it's on the stage or on a basketball court. Being so close in age has meant that they've all truly grown up together. They know each other inside and out, and even as they've grown and developed, that closeness and bond has remained very, very firm—and at this stage it's unlikely to ever become less.

Musically, Scott remains the band's leader. He's certainly the most accomplished musician, the one always ready to take a solo. He was a driving force in the change of direction that the brothers took, and he's extremely proud of everything they've achieved since their new beginning. It showed him that following his heart was definitely the right thing to do. Being the leader has also tended to make him the band's sex symbol. While he doesn't mind that too much, he does tend to make fun of it sometimes—he's up there as a musician, and he really wants to be taken seriously. Still, he knows they're there to entertain people; that's the bottom line.

All the adulation is great, but Scott's not letting it go to his head. At this point it would be easy for him to think of himself as a star, but that's not going to happen. In his own mind, he's simply another musician, and doesn't want to be "worshiped" the way some fans want to look up to him. "I don't want anybody to really worship anybody unless it's God," he says. So there's very little danger of him coming out of this with a swelled head. But Frank has always made sure his kids kept their feet very firmly planted on the ground, and had a firm grasp of what was real and what wasn't. Scott's learned his lessons very well.

His dedication to his art is so strong that, if he had to be stranded on a desert island, the first thing he'd grab is his guitar. Of course, it would be followed closely by his

CDs and a CD player. A girl to keep him company would have to wait until he'd rescued the other stuff.

Like his brothers, Scott's packed a lot of living into a few years. He's seen plenty of the world, and there's more he'll be able to view as time goes by. He's worked very hard, both as a singer, and learning to play, and he's taken his natural talent and made the most of it. He'd be the first to admit that he's still got a long way to go to fulfill his potential, but he's willing to take the time and make the effort so that happens. Success in a commercial and financial way is nice, but it's not the be-all and end-all by which Scott measures things. It's not impossible that in a few years he'll make a solo record. Not because he won't be getting along with his brothers, but because some of his ideas won't fit within the group format. As is apparent from a song like "Frustration," he's already experimenting.

But he'll balance all that with real life—eventually. Though he'd someday like to be married with a couple of kids, there's a long time, and many, many miles to go before that happens. For the moment it's all work, but when this round of touring is complete—somewhere close to the millennium—there'll be the chance to play for a while, to remember what it's like to be a teenager. Knowing Scott, however, he'll probably spend a lot of free time in his room, working up new material for the band . . . he's just so totally driven to do what he does.

They're all driven, really; it's just more obvious in Scott's case. He's the intense one of the group (no wonder his brothers make fun of him). But, of course, all the personalities mesh together so well that intensity can be good. In Scott's case, very good indeed.

Dave

Dave is the youngest of the triplets, if only by a few minutes. While Bob and Clint are identical twins, Dave is different (but just as cute as all the others). When he was born, he was the heaviest of the three, the biggest, but also the shortest. These days, though, he's grown more than a little, and he's the tallest of all the four brothers.

All of the triplets were born in Vancouver, British Columbia, and grew up just across the water in Victoria. When they were young, all of Dave's brothers used to tease him about being short, but he turned around and showed them. Even so, David Michael William Moffatt, as he was christened, isn't huge. He still only wears an eight-and-a-half shoe. The Big D nickname the others gave him dates back to his short days, although now it's somewhat ironic.

"He just eats and eats and it's his favorite thing to do," Clint says. "And then he got a little bit taller. We can't rub it in anymore."

He's also the once who excels academically in all the subjects. While the others have areas in which they shine, it's Dave who does really well all across the board. Will he go to college? That still remains to be seen. There's time to figure all that out yet; after all, he's just completed ninth grade, and a lot depends on the band carrying on playing—although, realistically, they're unlikely to ever stop. If he did go to college, it might well be to study music, since his ambition is "to become an accomplished keyboard player," and he knows that "I'll always be a musician."

While he's shy on the surface, once you get to know him, Dave is a real talker, "very, very gabby," as he describes himself—he can keep going at you forever, if you'll let him. He's particularly shy around girls, believe it or not. He's never had a girlfriend, at least not yet, anyway. He's always found it difficult to talk to a girl and ask her out on a date, although, if he were to do so, it would be to watch a movie, have dinner, and then perhaps go bowling. And what kind of meal would it be? Chinese food, probably, since that's his favorite.

Musically, Dave has a real love of melody, as is quite apparent from the way he uses his keyboards to fill out the sound of Scott's guitar, and to color the songs with his playing. So it's not too astonishing that his favorite musician is Sir Paul McCartney, the Beatles' bass player who used his bass so melodically, and who has also been such a prolific songwriter. In fact, the Beatles are still his very favorite band, with "Ob-la-di, Ob-la-da," which first appeared in 1968 on *The Beatles* (a.k.a. *The White Album*) as his all-time favorite song. With its Jamaican rhythm (the accent on the second and fourth beats, like reggae), it's an unusual song, and possibly it influenced what the boys did a little on "Say'n I Love U" even if that does owe rather more to the current crop of ska bands.

It would also help explain why his favorite song from *Chapter 1: A New Beginning* is "If Life is So Short." Just like Scott, it's the melody of it that appeals to him. Also the fact that it gives the brothers a real chance to shine on their harmonies. Dave may not be the lead voice on the songs, but he understands how much weight the harmonies carry in the Moffatts' sound.

And while his keyboard playing seems to take a secondary role to Scott's guitar work, don't be fooled into thinking he's just there for decoration. Take away his keyboards, and you lose a very important part of the music. He's a skilled musician, just like his other brothers, one who could play a lot more—if it were needed. What he understands is that the notes you play, or don't play, depend on what the song needs. Quite deliberately, the guitar is the main instrument in the Moffatts. Sure, Scott is the best player, but the others aren't far behind. Dave had several years of piano lessons. He can play classical as well as rock, and he can also manage some jazz. But his heart lies in the music he's playing now. The band is like four pieces of a jigsaw puzzle—remove one and it's incomplete.

Like the others, he's changed as he's grown older. If you look at the original cover of *Chapter 1: A New Beginning*, Dave has pretty short hair, parted in the middle, and a slightly goofy expression on his face. He's a little chubbier than the others. Less than a year later, he has a new hairstyle, a bit shorter, and much spikier—and much cooler—on top. He's finally grown into himself, a little thinner. They've all grown, of course, but the new 'do makes it far more obvious with Dave.

In a way, that's ironic, because he's always been the one who never cared about trends, unlike Scott, who has been really fashion-conscious for four years now. Dave was always the one who made his own decisions, who didn't really care too much about clothes and appearance—at least, any more than he had to, given that he made his living performing in public, and had to look good. Finally, though, it's as if being a teenager is catching up with him. Funnily enough, the others don't tease him about his short hair, although they really dump on Clint about his!

Of the four, he's the one who still most likes country music, and the biggest highlight of his life was when the Moffatts got to meet Garth Brooks, probably the biggest name in modern country music. They were on the same bill as the black-hatted one, back in their country days, and it was a chance for them to meet one of their idols. He was an absolute gentleman with them, polite, offering advice, while they, especially Dave, were in absolute awe of him. The guys had covered Brooks's song, "When God Made You" (which he'd co-written with Pat Alger on their self-titled debut) so they were naturally honored to meet him.

Dave's been lucky, and he knows it. There have been very few disappointments in his life—the biggest is the fact that the boys didn't get to sing the National Anthem at an L.A. Kings hockey game. Things could have been much, much worse. His biggest fear is of snakes. While he might encounter a few in Nashville, or perhaps on tour in Asia—although not in the hotels and stadiums where he spends most of his time—in Victoria and Germany snakes were very few and far between, and none of them particularly dangerous, and certainly not deadly. However, it means we shouldn't expect the Moffatts to introduce a snake into their stage act any time soon!

Although he left there when he was young, Dave has very strong and fond memories of Victoria. It's still one of his favorite places to spend time (although time is a very valuable commodity with him these days) when he has a chance for vacation. But he also likes places that are a lot warmer, with Florida ranking high on the list, just below Spain, which he describes as "definitely one of the most beautiful places I've seen."

Within the band, Dave has developed a rep for being the really kooky one, a bit of a goofball and a joker. But that's fine; every band needs one of those to keep its spirits up when things get boring on the road. And it's not as if he ever goes overboard.

He also has his quiet side. It's not common knowledge, but Dave is something of an artist. Everywhere goes, pencils and a sketch pad go with him (he'd even take them to a desert island, along with a book and a radio . . . oh, and a girl). On tour, the sketch pad lives on the seat next to him, so he can just pick it up and put down his impression of a place or a person that he's just seen. It helps occupy his time, and it also helps develop the other talent he has. Maybe in time Dave will end up doing all the designs for the band's album covers—it could easily happen.

For now, and always, it's really the music that matters, though. Scott might be the group leader, but all the brothers have an equal say in the writing and arranging of their songs, and Dave is slowly playing a bigger role instrumentally. Just listen to "Over the Rainbow" and you can hear how it's his keyboard that drives the riff. It won't be long before he's taking some solos, and easing the weight off Scott's shoulders a little bit. After all, he has the other possible lead instrument in the band, and he can provide additional coloring to the sound, and the keyboard has a wider range of sounds than the guitar.

Essentially, being a part of this band is all he's ever known in his life. He was the one who got them all started, when he picked up his mother's microphone on the stage in Victoria. If not for that single incident, the Moffatts might not be where they are today. So since he was four years old, Dave has been a performer, absolutely loving it.

But performing doesn't make for a totally rounded life, even when there's drawing to fill the empty moments. Dave does have a few other interests. He's into movies, although he's yet to take a girl to see one. His favorites are *Scream* (the first one) and *Titanic*. Neither of those films has his favorite actors, however. Among males, he likes to watch Bruce Willis, since Bruce tends to go for the all-action kind of film, which Dave also enjoys. Among the women, though, it's not a babe like Jennifer Love Hewitt who really floats his boat, but instead the sweetness of Sandra Bullock.

And he wouldn't be a Moffatt if he didn't get into some sports. Perhaps it's a legacy of spending some time in Europe, where the game is huge: he's a soccer fan, and supported Germany during the 1998 World Cup. But in America, you're more than likely to find him shooting hoops with some guys from his old neighborhood in Nashville. He also loves to go swimming. It's something easily done in Florida and Spain, but to go sea swimming in Victoria isn't that easy—more often than not, the water's too cold. However, when they're on the road, and staying in hotels with pools, it's the perfect exercise.

Given a bit of free time, you might just find Dave at the fishing hole. It might sound unlikely, but it's true. He likes to get out into the country (even though he can't drive yet) and spend a day with a rod and reel, just relaxing and seeing what he can catch. As a way of clearing all the stress of touring from his mind, there's nothing better. And if he can take a book along, put the line in the water, and just spend the day in the sun, reading, there could be absolutely nothing finer.

That free time is very rare these days, however, and home, he knows, tends to be whatever hotel room they're in that night. It's an exciting life, and one that keeps him very close to his family, the only people he sees every single day. And it would be easy for him to begin to think of himself as a star, because all the girls are screaming for him. Like his other brothers, though, Dave never does that. He's genuinely grateful to see the fans, that they would buy the records, and pay to see the band perform live. The only real difference between him and the fans is simply that he's the one up on the stage, playing. He has talent, but he knows that a lot of the fans do, and that only talent, perseverance, and a hefty dose of luck have gotten him where he is today.

As for the future, it's always going to be music, even if he should take time out for college. Music moves him more than anything else, even if it does mean he has a rootless kind of existence. He'll be a part of the Moffatts for as long as they're together (the band, that is; obviously the family will never break up). He doesn't need to shine, or be the front man, the real entertainer. His surface shyness means that he's quite content in the background, singing the harmonies and providing the keyboard playing. Maybe in time he'll start doing sessions for other bands, or possibly some production work. The guys have produced some of their own tracks, and they understand how a recording studio works. The solo album route is unlikely for Dave. It would thrust him too much into the spotlight, which isn't the most comfortable place for him. When he's up there with his brothers, that's one thing. But to do it all on his own would be a different matter.

Being part of a set of triplets is a strange bond for him. He has two very close brothers, but at the same time, with them being identical twins, he's also kind of the odd man out. He doesn't share the telepathic connection of the twins, but neither is he separate and older, like Scott. It's an odd position, not quite one thing, and not the other, either, which might help account for that initial shyness. But there's absolutely no doubt that he's a member of the Moffatt family, where it's all for one and one for all. The family is the base of his life. It couldn't be any other way for him. The whole crew is tight in a way most families only dream about. They've experienced everything together, had the kind of adventures and travel that usually only seem to occur on television. They've even been schooled at home (although Frank has been considering hiring a tutor to take over the teaching duties).

There's no doubt that in the Moffatts, every piece, every member, is as important as every other member. And just because you're shy doesn't mean you're not vital. Dave's ambitions as a musician, to become the very best keyboard player he can be, do him justice. As they all improve, and grow, and learn more, the possibilities for them all—individually and together—will be absolutely massive. You can bet that Dave's name will still be there ten, even twenty years from now. And that he'll still be having the time of his life—playing music.

Clint

Clinton Thomas John Moffatt is one half of the identical-twin duo of Clint and Bob, who were born, along with Dave, in Vancouver, British Columbia, on March 8, 1984. In a way, having identical twins as a band's rhythm section (bass and drums) is perfect. They're already in sync with each other, and that's what you need for the heart and soul of any group.

Just in case you didn't know, Clint is the one with the *really* short hair in the band (and no, he's never regretted cutting it that way), and with the blond bangs. Of course, Scott also has blond bangs, but given the difference in hair length, there's no mistaking the two of them! He's also the foil to Scott onstage. The two of them are the ones who are free to move around as they play, and they make the most of it, Clint with his white bass that flashes brightly under the stage lights.

He's the one who brings the real rock influence into the band. While his all-time favorite band is the Beatles, his favorite album and song both come from Bryan Adams (*Reckless* and "Heaven," respectively), another hometown boy from British Columbia who made it to super-stardom. You can hear it in the way he plays, underpinning everything. He never tries to overpower any of the songs to show off his virtuosity—and he is a very good bass player—but instead contributes just what the song needs, working closely with Bob to ensure the rhythm and the beat remain strong, or subtle, as necessary. Knowing what *not* to play, and leaving space, is every bit as important as being able to play fast. Then again, given the fact that Clint's ambition is "to become the best musician I can be," perhaps it's not too surprising. He's been playing long enough to have an understanding of what works and what doesn't. And given his love of rock 'n' roll, it's not totally astonishing that his favorite song on *Chapter 1: A New Beginning* is the very uptempo "Say'n I Love U," which gives him a good workout on the bass, playing those bouncy ska bass lines! But it's only natural for the different members of a band to bring their own influences to the music they make, even if they are brothers. "Musically there are a lot of differences, which is great for a band," Clint says.

When he was born, Clint had a hernia, a condition not completely uncommon in babies, and solved with an operation. That meant he had to stay in hospital in Vancouver while his brothers went home to Victoria, across the water. The night of his operation was the first sign of the amazing non-verbal communication he shared with his twin. At the time the operation finished, in the wee small hours, Bob woke in the family home and began crying, for no apparent reason. It was only later they discovered what had happened.

Then, when they were both little more than toddlers, Clint was hit in the head by a baseball bat while playing. He had a minor concussion and had to be taken to hospital, and was kept in overnight for observation. He awoke, in pain, in the middle of the night. At exactly the same time, at home, Bob woke up, too!

All that made the family realize the special quality the two of them shared, but it took a long time to convince their teachers. During the time they attended school (before Frank took over their home schooling), the teachers were convinced they were copying from each other, because they always came up with exactly the same answers—and always picked the same questions. There was only one way to prove that wasn't the case, and that was to put them in separate rooms and give them the same test. The results proved what Clint and Bob already knew—they thought exactly the same way. Finally, the teachers understood, and let them be.

As they've grown up, however, they've become more individual, as is always the case. With their very different hairstyles, Clint and Bob are easily distinguished from each other, although their faces really still are the same (take a picture, try holding your hand over their hair and then tell the difference between them). And their personalities, too, have changed. Clint got into fashion before any of the others. When he was younger, he didn't care what he wore, but after that, he quite seriously asked his parents to buy him suits for Christmas. He liked getting dressed up and looking good. Which might go some way toward explaining why he's also the real neat freak of the bunch. As Bob described him, Clint might get up at four A.M., remake his bed—with hospital corners—then get back into it, and go back to sleep. Not many people would do that! Even on tour, everything has to be absolutely in order for him. And that's quite a task, considering just how much time he spends on the road.

Seeing so much of the world really has given him a different outlook on life. There are certain cities he loves to visit, especially Barcelona, Spain, and London, England, but give him some free time, and he'd be much happier heading for Dallas, Texas, or Destin, Florida, his two favorite places in the world. In other words, he likes to be where he's hot (maybe because he's a hottie himself). And how many fifteen-year-olds would have seen so much of the globe that they'd have difficulty thinking of where their favorite places might be, having so many to choose from?

Clint likes to keep very active. At just over five feet, three inches, basketball isn't his best sport, but he does play a lot of football and soccer. Like Dave, he enjoys swimming, the easiest exercise when on tour. And, also like

Dave, he likes to get away and go fishing for a day—anything that gets him around nature. His other great love is a sport a lot of musicians seem to like, although it's more associated with oldies, and that's golf. It seems hard to imagine him dressed in a lot of loud plaid and polyester walking around a golf course, but you never know—you might want to keep your eyes open next time you're driving by the country club, just in case Clint is in your town and enjoying a quick eighteen holes.

When it comes to girls, Clint has a bit more experience than Dave, but not a whole lot. He's never had a steady relationship, although he has dated several times. Right now, of course, a relationship is totally out of the question—he's never in one place long enough to really get to know someone. And these days, he's a little wary of girls. If he's going to see someone, it has to be someone who's interested in him for who he is, not because he's one of the Moffatts. That's really important, and sometimes it can be hard to figure out someone's motives—after all, these guys get girls throwing themselves at them constantly. So, for now, it's easier to remain single. Although, just in case you're imagining Clint isn't obsessed with the opposite sex, check this out—his favorite word in the English language (actually in any language) is "girls." So you can tell what he's thinking about a lot of the time.

If he were to go out on a date, though, it would be dinner and a movie. Preferably a scary movie, "because your date will cling to you when she got frightened." And that seems reasonable enough. The one thing he'd have to remember, though, when they're out, would be to not indulge his bad habit.

Yes, Clint does have one bad habit. He cracks his knuckles. Now, there are plenty of worse things in the world, but at the wrong moment, it can be pretty gross. Nothing like a cracking knuckle to destroy a romantic moment. But, being the sensitive type, he'd never do anything like that—he'd wait until he was around his brothers. People have warned him that cracking those knuckles will make them big, but he doesn't want to hear it. He also snaps his fingers a lot, but he's a musician, so it's allowed. . . .

And if he *did* take a girl out to dinner, chances are it would be to a Mexican restaurant, since his favorite foods are "Mexican cooking and pizza." But first he'd have to make sure he had money with him. Normally he doesn't carry very much. In fact, during one interview, when asked what he had in his pockets, the sum total was his wallet and a laser pointer—not even any change!

Like Dave, he was absolutely thrilled when the Moffatts met Garth Brooks. Although they've met other famous people before and since, Brooks was the absolute standout, and he's certainly been one of the biggest stars of the Nineties, someone the boys can look up to. And he remains an inspiration, even if they guys aren't playing country music any more. They believe they can be as big as he is. And, the way things are going, they may well be right. Brooks is massive in North America, but once you get beyond the continent, he's just another name. The only place the Moffatts aren't huge—yet—is America. And that will change very soon.

One person he'd love to meet is his favorite movie star, comedian Jim Carrey (who, coincidentally, is yet another Canadian who's made it big in the States). Clint might like to take his dates to scary movies, but if he's sitting down on his own to watch something, there's a good chance he'll pull out his video of *Ace Ventura, Pet Detective* to screen again. It doesn't matter how many times he sees it, he still loves it (and the sequel, too). Like a lot of other people, he thinks Carrey's manic, over-the-top humor and rubber face are just hilarious. When it comes to female stars, however, he's exactly like his brother Dave, and adores the sweetness of Sandra Bullock—and who can blame him? From *Speed* onward, she's been a total babe on screen, one who brings out the romantic in all guys.

Sensitive as he is, though, Clint remains resolutely male in one respect. Asked by an interviewer when he'd last cried, Clint thought for a minute and answered, "Honestly,

I can't remember." Then again, he hasn't had too much to cry about, really. Life has been pretty good to him, and that doesn't look like it's going to change. In fact, the way things have been lately, the only tears are likely to be those of joy. One day he'd like to have a house with a play room, or den, which he could fill with all the band's platinum records and awards. And he'll very likely have it. He could already afford the house, but somehow the idea of Clint living on his own wouldn't sit well with his dad or stepmom! And of course, he still loves being around his brothers.

While the triplets seemed very much like triplets when they were younger, as they've grown that feeling has changed. Now, according to Clint, "We don't even consider ourselves triplets, until someone asks about it." And that's understandable. As they've grown, and they've acquired their own interests, they've become more individual. But the family bond remains, and there'll always be something very special and telepathic between Clint and Bob; it's unavoidable. They'll know when the other is in trouble or in pain, even if they're on the other side of the world. But that's the way it should be.

There's a lot of fun ahead for Clint. A whole world of girls, and a whole world of music. Drop him on a desert island with his bass, a hammock, and a girl, and you'd have a happy camper, with the best of everything. Well, he'd be happy for a while, anyway . . . until he got the urge to start playing shows again, anyway.

As with the rest of his brothers, Clint doesn't want to stay still musically. This album is a starting point, but they'll continue to evolve with each new record. Each of them has something they bring to the band, and to the songs they write together. In Clint's case, his bass playing is the heartbeat of each tune, while his voice is an essential part of the harmony. He's the one who helps them to rock out and to underpin the melody, giving it the bottom end.

The other thing about being on the stage is that it gives him an outlet for all that energy. He moves around a *lot*, bouncing off Scott, teasing the fans a little, but playing all the while. Each show is like playing a game of basketball or soccer with the amount of running around he does. But don't except to see him (or any of the others) bungee-jumping on the stage. He's like the others—the one time they tried it, it scared him half to death, and he's not about to give it another shot.

Extrovert, always smiling, Clint helps keep everyone's spirits up when they're on tour. When bad things happen, it depresses him, but he soon snaps out of it and is happy again, trying to make sure everyone else is, too. If there were ever a fight between the brothers, it would probably be Clint who'd end up as the peacemaker in the group. He knows the pressure they're all under (and while it seems like a lot of fun, doing what they do, there is a lot of pressure, also) and does all he can to ensure it doesn't become too much for everybody. A month of traveling and playing shows might seem like a great time, but the reality is a lot harsher—it's essentially a month without a good night's sleep, and always searching for a good meal and clean clothes.

So what should we expect from Clint in the future? A lot, probably. His musical commitment remains the Moffatts, but it's likely he'll do what he can to help other young bands along and get them signed. He loves to play, and it wouldn't be too unlikely to see him sit in and jam with other bands, just for the experience of it. The future holds a lot of possibilities for him, but inevitably he'll remain connected to music in one form or another, primarily as the Moffatts' bass player. In time . . . well, who knows? But it's a sure bet that as long as the band continues playing, Clint will be up there with them, relishing every single second of it, and tearing into the music like there's no tomorrow.

Bob

So who is Robert Franklin Peter Moffatt, anyway? Well, he's the oldest—if only by a minute or two—of the triplets, and the identical twin of Clint. He's the guy who keeps the beat in the band, the one behind the drum kit, or, on the ballads, softly tapping the congas and percussion. Without him there, it just wouldn't be the same. That telepathic communication he shares with his bass-playing brother makes them into one of music's perfect rhythm sections. He feels his brother's pain, and vice versa, something they've understood since they were tiny, even if it took others a while to pick up on what was happening. "Duke," as the others call him (don't ask why!), is the one who likes to please everyone. He's Mr. Cooperative, the one whose ambition is "to make everyone happy," something he seems to be fulfilling with the Moffatts. Certainly a lot of people go home from their shows feeling very good.

If Clint brings the rock influence into the band, Bob is the one who likes all the trappings of metal. His favorite musician, not surprisingly, is a drummer—Lars Ulrich, of Metallica (whose wife, by the way, used to be movie star Matt Damon's girlfriend), and his all-time favorite album is Metallica's *Black Album*, one of the best metal records of the Nineties, and light years away from the big-hair metal lite that seemed to fill the Eighties. Listen closely to Clint and you can understand what he's learned from listening to Ulrich. He hits hard, but knows he doesn't have to fill every space with a sound. He can propel a song by using a strong backbeat—which is always the best way, since it gets people's feet moving, which is what the band really wants. And, of course, he's one of those singing drummers, wearing a headset to allow him to add his voice to the harmonies while he plays. Like all his brothers, Bob has a very good voice, and he keeps it lubricated on stage with apple soda or water (when he's not on stage, though, he likes to drink apple soda or Coke). As a singer, he really admires Matchbox 20, whose song "Push" remains his favorite single—understandably, since it uses the voices and the drums in a very creative way. He's always listening, and always working to improve his technique. Like the others, his life revolves around music. He eats, sleeps, breathes, and even dreams it. He's one of four brothers who are absolutely driven by what they hear in their heads. Curiously, given the type of music he loves, his personal favorite on *Chapter 1: A New Beginning* is "If Life is So Short." But, then again, the majority of the brothers love that one, and it is a very classy piece of pop music that does frame their vocal skills particularly well.

Like his brothers, Bob totally believes in the band, and he'd love to see them on the cover of *Rolling Stone* one day. That's very far from ridiculous—Britney Spears has been there, and the magazine is starting to acknowledge the new pop music. And, to go along with the single of "Until You Loved Me," the guys have a video out, which is going to get them more widely known. Big-time fame is just around the corner, and *Rolling Stone* is a strong possibility. They've already been in all the teen magazines, including *Teen People*, and a number of Canadian publications have written about them.

Since Bob also loves to watch MTV (and, when he's in Germany, Viva, the German equivalent of MTV), he's probably going to be seeing a lot of himself in the months to come. Or he may decide to surf a little and catch some sports—the other big thing in his life. When he was young he played some ice hockey, the way many Canadian boys do, and even won a trophy for it. He doesn't often play these days, but he can often be found tossing a football around, or kicking a soccer ball. Fishing is up there, too, when he wants to relax, and, like Clint, he enjoys golf—to play, not to watch. Actually, playing sports is his favorite way of spending his free time, although that time has become very limited.

It seems as if the triplets have very similar taste in female movie stars: Like the other two, Bob loves Sandra Bullock. But when it comes to male movie stars, Bob goes for the suave action-hero type—Sean Connery, the original James Bond of the movies. Neither of those fit in with his all-time favorite films, however. He can be a sucker for *Titanic* if he's in a romantic mood, but the ones that really do it for him are *The Jackal* and *Scream*. If it can scare him, then he's happy.

But on a perfect evening, he wouldn't take his date to a scary movie. Instead it would be a candlelit dinner, "then some ice cream afterwards." Then, maybe, the chance to go bowling. Which wouldn't be too bad at all. Of course, he's had the opportunity to do that, since, for three years, while he lived in Nashville, he did have a girlfriend named Maria. By some strange twist of fate, her parents moved—to Canada, Bob's homeland, and that kind of ended the relationship. In some ways, it might have been for the best, since Bob really doesn't have the time to give to a relationship now. Still, he and Maria remain "good friends."

Like Scott, Bob enjoys wearing his hair long, and parted down the middle, flowing onto his shoulders, he looks just a little bit like another drummer (well, former drummer)—Dave Grohl, of the Foo Fighters. Without ever being vain, Bob is concerned with always looking his best, although he's tended to stay away from the baggy look—check out the single of "Until You Loved Me" and you'll see him stylin' in jeans with massive cuffs. This is a guy who understands what's happening in clothes, and thoroughly enjoys it. At the same time, he's not a sheep, blindly following every trend that comes along. He knows what suits him, and wears that. Sure, a part of it is that he *has* to look good, being a performer, but it's also because he honestly enjoys it, although he's nowhere near the clotheshorse Scott is. Still, this is a guy who considers "a suitcase full of clothes" to be essential when traveling. Along with his CD player and his drums, of course—well, he wouldn't do too well on tour without his drums! And a pair of drumsticks would be something he'd take to the proverbial desert island (actually, he'd take the whole drum kit if he could).

Bob has developed over the years into a very solid drummer. He does exactly what a drummer should, keeping things moving without trying to hog the instrumental spotlight, working with Clint to provide a very strong framework for each song. For him, as for the rest of his brothers, it's all about the song, making sure that gets across. They may play their personal brand of pop-rock, and their harmonies may carry the ballads, but if you can't hear the song, then there's no point to it. And Bob doesn't need to be the front man; he's content to leave that to Scott (and to a lesser degree, Clint). He can clown around with the rest of them, but underneath he's the more serious type, a little quieter and more reserved. Singing harmony, rather than lead, is perfect for him, and having a drum set to hide behind works well (he's also the only one who gets to sit down while he's working, too!). But check out his arms sometime—all those years of playing and hitting things have given him some pretty impressive biceps.

It's not surprising that music is the central thing in his life—it would be worrying if it weren't, really. But the other big part of every single day is family. Bob knows his brothers—especially Clint, better than anyone in the world, and like the other three, he's closer to his parents than most teenagers ever are. In fact, when asked to describe his relationship with Frank and Sheila, he was able to sum it up in five words: "Happy, cool, hard, affectionate, sublime," which is about as strongly positive as you're ever going to find—and how many fifteen-year-olds could say the same thing?

Bob is the one the others turn to when it comes to figures. He always been good at math, and working things out—for once, just the opposite of his twin, who excels in literature. But the two of them have been slowly diverging for a few years now, finding their individuality and ways of expressing it, and differentiating themselves from each other. There's still that telepathy, of course, which won't ever vanish, but they've grown into themselves. They still share interests in some things, like comedies and scary movies, but overall they've become quite different. There's no danger of them being mistaken for clones any more!

They do both share a love of Florida, though. Naples is Bob's favorite vacation destination in the U.S., although he also thoroughly enjoys going "home" to Victoria, British Columbia, to see family and old, old friends. Not too amazingly, given the fact that his grandparents are just across the water in Vancouver, it's the place where he gets really spoiled and indulged. Give him his choice of anywhere in the world, however, and he'll get straight on a plane for London. He loves the busy streets, the shopping, the accents and the "good atmosphere" (a very English phrase creeping into his language there!). Of course, given the fact that Victoria was once supposed to be more English than England, it's no wonder he feels right at home there! Actually, since he loves to travel so much, just put him on a plane anywhere, and he's quite content. Seeing the world, and the way people live, is one of his fascinations. Nowadays, as his face is known in more and more places, it's getting harder for him to just walk about and see things, though.

London is also a place he might be able to run into three of his heros, the trio he'd love to meet over everyone else—Sir Paul McCartney, Ringo Starr, and George Harrison, the three surviving members of the Beatles (John Lennon was killed in 1980). They're his very favorite band, and they're heroes to millions of people around the world, even though it's just about thirty years since they stopped existing as a band—now that's longevity! But it's understandable how Bob could feel that way. Either directly or indirectly, they've had an influence on every band that's come along since. You can't play music and not be aware of their work—you can't even listen to the radio and not know about them. The melody in the Moffatts' songs has a lot to do with what they've learned listening to the Beatles, having been introduced to the music by Frank. It's there in the chord changes and the harmonies. And the band doesn't mind one bit; they're happy to owe a debt to people they consider the best.

Of course, Bob wouldn't be human if he didn't have at least one bad habit, and his is the one he shares with his twin—cracking his knuckles. Like the rest of the guys, he's totally anti-smoking and anti-drug. When you're as active as Bob is, you don't want to do things that will just slow you down and make you lose control. Bob has been gifted with the ability to make music, just like his other brothers, and he doesn't take it for granted. He certainly doesn't abuse it, and he never will. He also actively encourages all the band's fans—well, everybody, really—to stay away from cigarettes and drugs.

It's been a wonderful life so far for Bob, and it just seems likely to get better and better. The Moffatts have had some very good breaks, but they've also backed them up with plenty of talent, and the willingness to work very hard and take advantage of every opportunity that's come their way. Musically Bob is way ahead of most fifteen-year-old boys. Those few who can play drums are most likely still banging away in their parents' basement, or playing in a garage band, not performing to thousands of screaming girls on stages all over the world. But Bob accepts success calmly, even philosophically. He understands luck has played a part, and always will. He's also looking ahead, to the way the band will develop in the future. Not that they'll end up sounding like his beloved Metallica—it's doubtful you'll ever hear a metal version of the Moffatts on record—

but there's still so much they can explore. But who knows—if they take some time off, maybe Bob will put a metal band together to exercise the thrashing side of his personality. He'd have a great time doing it, and with his professional experience you know they'd be good, even to non-metalheads.

Mostly, though, his focus will remain with the band. It's not just his family, it's his life. It's a 24/7 thing, and with America just opening up to them, there's still plenty of work to be done, as well as keeping the name very much alive in other parts of the world. Between shows, promotion, interviews, and everything else, Bob has to be one of the four busiest people on the planet right now. And that's going to continue indefinitely.

If you think of the brothers as the Four Musketeers, you're coming very close to the way things really are. They might tease each other, and argue from time to time, but in reality they're one very solid unit, made up of four individuals, all related by blood. They're tight with each other, and they'd always defend each other (and remember they're all trained in kung fu, too!). It's all for one and one for all. Always has been, and always will be, for as long as they live. The band is their outlet, their life, their career and their hobby. Everything fits together so well, it just had to be that way.

PART FOUR
THE LAST BIT

On The Horizon

If anyone has a bright future these days, it has to be the Moffatts. America is just waiting for them (even if some bits of the country haven't had a chance to realize it yet), and pop-rock is going to be the soundtrack to the millennium. They've been making friends everywhere they go—and they've still got a few places to travel.

In Germany they've really achieved superstar status. They were one of the bands asked to take part in the recording of a charity single, "Let the Music Heal Your Soul," under the name of the *Bravo* All-Stars—and only people who had the biggest names in Germany were asked to help out. They also were featured on the latest single by German singing star Gil. "If You Only Knew" had very prominent vocals by all four of the Moffatts, not to mention their picture on the inside of the sleeve. Then again, they also helped to write the song, along with Gil Ofarim himself. It's a sign of just how big they were there when "featuring the Moffatts" becomes a major selling point on the cover of a single. They were also in the video for the song, and Scott said that "shooting with Gil was cool."

If they can do that in Europe, think of the possibilities for America. A collaboration with Hanson, perhaps? Working with Britney Spears? But that's the beauty of music—anything's possible.

The brothers have come a long, long way. Not just geographically, but musically, and they've learned with every single step that they've taken. From playing charity shows in British Columbia to performing for ten thousand screaming fans in Asia is a huge change. Still, life is about taking chances. And the brothers took a major one. They could have continued with their country career and made a very comfortable living. Selling three hundred thousand copies of *The Moffatts* wasn't just peanuts.

Instead, they showed real courage and walked into the unknown, to play the music that was in their hearts. You have to admire anyone who's willing to stand up for what they believe, and this band did it in a major way. No one had any idea if what they were doing was really commercial. It was all just hope and a very great deal of faith in themselves. Yes, it paid off, but it might not have done. The fact that they were willing to take that chance, to turn their back on established success to do what they wanted to do, sets them apart from a lot of people. They showed guts.

And they've persevered, too. They've worked their butts of all around the globe. Having a hit was just the beginning of that new chapter. From there they had to let people know who they were, and that meant long, grueling treks all around the globe. To be sure, playing was big fun, and the traveling itself was exciting for the guys, but there was also the sheer daily tedium. But they weren't about to let that get them down. They were on a mission; there was a world to conquer.

It's ironic that America is the last place to get the Moffatts. Their sound is *so* American (even if they are Canadian), that in some ways they should have broken here first. But pop music was out of style—and more points to the band for playing what they loved, not what was fashionable—and no one wanted to know. Now everyone is falling over themselves to talk to the boys, to help them along. But that's how it goes in show business—certainly on the business side of things.

Like Hanson—whom they inspired—the Moffatts will

show a generation of young bands that it really is possible to be teenagers and have your music taken seriously. Obviously there's much more to it than just getting up on the stage and having hordes of girls screaming. There are quite a few years of work to be put in before all that happens. You have to know how to play your instrument well, and how to write songs. You've got to know where you want to go. In short, you've got to pay your dues. The boys paid theirs on the country circuit. Look back and you'll see how they built it all up. They started with nothing, unknown, no record out, and things got bigger and better each year. From charity gigs in Victoria to playing Vegas was a big jump, but they'd made the transition gradually. And thanks had to go to the Osmonds, who encouraged another family, and offered them help and support, not to mention a long-running gig in Branson.

There's a saying, actually the motto of the British Special Air Service: "Who dares wins." The Moffatts, under Frank's guiding hand, have always dared. They dared to go to Branson, then to Las Vegas, and then to Nashville. At the time, those were all big moves, bold moves, all or nothing moves. Every one paid off. And in making them, Frank imbued in his kids the right idea, that you have to be willing to take chances, to stake everything sometimes. From an early age the brothers have known that this is what they were born to do. "We plan to be playing music forever" is what they say, and after doing it for a decade, it's easy to believe.

They're serious about all this—that's never been in doubt. They want respect for what they do, and they deserve it. Listen to the album, go and see them in concert, and it's them playing the instruments, rocking out the house, not a backing tape. Every show is slightly different. The covers they do—ranging from Collective Soul to the Police to the Beatles—reflect their wide-ranging interest in music. These are four guys who are just totally in love with what they do.

"There really aren't a lot of acts like us right now,"

says Scott, "that play music, real music, play instruments, and write their own songs." He's right. It helps set them apart, and makes it all way more personal. And with songs "about fun, parties, and relationships, whatever comes to our mind" there's plenty of ground to cover.

Perhaps the biggest question isn't where have they been, but where will they go. The Moffatts keep developing at a rapid pace. For now, they're being compared to Hanson, that other band of brothers, but it won't be long before people are mentioning Oasis and Van Halen, two other bands containing brothers (although Bob, Scott, Clint, and Dave get along much better than Liam and Noel Gallagher, it has to be said). What will happen with their music is pretty much anyone's guess—they probably don't really know themselves—but the chances are that it will always have a big element of pop music in it. A good chorus and sweet harmonies are things that they love, that crop up in most things they write.

Of course, there are exceptions to that, pointing in other directions, and giving them outlets for other emotions, and other styles. Will we see Bob directing a metal B-side for the band? Why not? There are lots of directions open to them as they continue to grow. In another decade they may prove to be one of the most respected bands on the planet. In a record company press release, "Until You Loved Me" was referred to as an "I Wanna Hold your Hand" (a reference to the song that made the Beatles big stars in America in 1964) for the millennium. That was undoubtedly a bit of hype, but maybe not too far off the mark. In 1964 the Beatles were still finding their feet. In the next six years they literally changed the face of popular music. And the time is right for another band to do it again. Why shouldn't it be the Moffatts? They have all the skills in their hands, hearts, and minds. They have a fan base who'll follow them wherever they go musically. And they have the imagination and the ambition. Everything is in place, and time will provide the answer on that one.

For now, though, they're pop stars, and they're happy

with that, even if they're not always comfortable with all the adulation. They have a very realistic sense of who they are, that they're very human and not the gods all their fans make them out to be. After doing this for so long, they're not about to get carried away by all the screaming and the praise, which is very commendable in boys aged sixteen and fifteen, since boys that age can often get carried away. No one in this band is going to get an inflated idea of himself. For a start, the others, including Frank, would never let it happen, and the impulse just isn't there in the first place. Raised right, they've learned their lessons.

They're professionals at what they do. By now they couldn't be anything less. Although they don't go to too many shows themselves, they know what they'd like to see, and give that to their audiences. And everyone seems to go home happy. Pop music is an international language. It transcends all the barriers—race, color, religion. You just have to understand the words to get the feel and know the message. Scott, Dave, Clint, and Bob are also very positive people. A couple of their songs might speak of alienation and feeling alone, outside, but they're very much involved in life, and enjoying every single minute of it. There aren't enough hours in the day to accommodate all the things they want to do.

With all the touring ahead of them, they've even sold the house they owned in Nashvile, since they're never there any more. So, for the moment, all of the Moffatts are literally homeless, although they're looking at making Vancouver their home base again, once the next stretch of touring is complete and they have the time to think again.

Over the summer of 1999, America is going to get very familiar with the Moffatts. They're going to be everywhere, on television, radio, the Net, and they'll be appearing all over the place performing. Call it a blitz if you want, but basically it's just giving the country a chance to catch up with the global phenomenon. England, too, will get its share of Moffatt mania, while Canada will get another dose. It's a full court press, and that's just fine. America might finally be ready for the good stuff, to remember that rock 'n' roll and guitars aren't bad things by any means. Expect the concerts to sell out quickly, because it's already happening. If you have *any* doubt as to how big this band is, check out their official Website (URL at the end of the book). They have links to all the Moffatts sites, official and fan—and there are more than *one hundred and ninety* of them. Not exactly what you'd call shabby, is it? You can spend a long time surfing around in Moffatt space and learn an awful lot. It's notable, too, that both the band and Capitol, their label in the U.S., are happy to include fans and their sites to help publicize the band—a pleasant change from those bands who seem to do everything possible to shut down the unofficial sites. They understand that it's the fans who are the backbone of it all, and who help the band become huge.

Cute will get you so far, but you need talent to back it up. The Moffatts have the babe-o-licious factor, but they also have the rest. They've got everything they need for total world domination. And that's not crazy—it's virtually already happened.

There's a long road ahead of the Moffatts, but now it's all freeway. The tolls have been paid, and they can put the pedal to the metal and go full speed ahead. It's going to be interesting to look back in, say, five years, and wonder how far they've come; the chances are it'll be a long, long way indeed.

The hits will keep on coming, along with the tours. There'll be fresh, exciting music, and who knows what else ... but that's down the line. Right now is the biggie. Having spent a long time waiting for June 8, 1999, the date *Chapter 1: A New Beginning* appeared, they could relax, and do what they did best—entertain the crowds live and in person. The video for "Until You Loved Me," directed by Nick Egan showed what they were about, and helped open the door. But it was always going to be the music that convinced everybody, songs you simply couldn't resist. One-hit wonders? Not a chance, not with the depth of talent and their background. This is what they're committed to, and even if the hits should ever dry up, they'll keep playing music, whether it's for several thousand in an arena, or a couple of hundred in a club.

Life is good when you're making your living doing something you enjoy. You're willing to endure a lot to keep doing it. The bad times don't seem so bad, and the good times seem totally brilliant. And if the people you're doing it for love it, that's even better. To get a positive reaction when you're on the stage, playing your music, is the wickedest buzz in the world. That's what happens every single time the Moffatts play a show, whether it's in Manila, Dusseldorf, or in your town.

Will they replace boy bands like BSB and 'N Sync? No, of course not. But there's plenty of room for more than one kind of music. They aren't even in direct competition—the styles are totally different. You won't find any R&B or hip-hop in the Moffatts' sound, for a start, and that's apart from the obvious instrument factor. They're just a different kind of boy band, self-contained, and with a different emphasis.

But they don't take it for granted that America will fall at their feet, the way the rest of the world has. In fact, they're remarkably modest about it. "We want to do what we love . . . and we just have to hope the public enjoys it."

Then again, there was never really much doubt about that, was there?

The Moffatts are here to stay.

Discography

Albums

What A Wonderful World

What a Wonderful World/ Grandma/ We're Off to the Rodeo/ All I Have is a Dream/ Itty Bitty Smile/ Bird Dog/ I Think I'm Falling in Love/ Dogs is Dogs/ Do Wah Diddy Diddy/ That's All Right

A Moffatts' Christmas

Old Man Winter/ The Brightest Star/ Earl the Christmas Squirrel/ The Greatest Gift/ Santa's in My Neighborhood/ How Would Jesus Feel?/ Oh What a Wonderful Day/ Santa Knows/ Christmas Eve/ Santa Left a Hole in Daddy's Pocket

The Moffatts

I Think She Likes Me/ This Boy/ Guns of Love/ Mama Never Told Me 'Bout You/ Just Thinkin' About You/ When God Made You/ Caterpillar Crawl/ You Are What You Do/ A Little Something/ Don't Judge This Book

Chapter 1: A New Beginning

Wild at Heart/ Miss You Like Crazy/ Say'n I Love U/ Girl of My Dreams/ Crazy/ Don't Walk Away/ Now and Forever/ Love/ I'll Be There for You/ Girl I'm Gonna Get you/ We Are Young/ If Life is So Short/ Jump/ Frustration (hidden bonus track)

Chapter 1: A New Beginning (U.S. Version)

Wild at Heart/ Miss You Like Crazy/ Say'n I Love U/ Girl of My Dreams/ Crazy/ Don't Walk Away/ Now and Forever/ Love/ I'll Be There for You/ Girl I'm Gonna Get You/ We Are Young/ If Life is So Short/ Jump/ Until You Loved Me/ Written All Over My Heart/ Misery/ Raining in My Mind

Singles

U.S.

Until You Loved Me/ Snippets of Misery/ Written All Over My Heart/ Miss You Like Crazy/ Let's Party

ELSEWHERE IN THE WORLD

I'll Be There for You/ Girl of My Dreams (Single Version)/ Girl of My Dreams (Live)/ Over the Rainbow (Garage Recording)/ Crazy/ Ya Ya/ Lara My Love/ I'll Be There For You (Radio Edit)/ I'll Be There for You (Long Version)/ I'll Be There for You (Instrumental)/ Now and Forever/ Miss You Like Crazy (Radio Edit)/ Miss You Like Crazy (Long Ver-

THE MOFFATTS

sion)/ Miss You Like Crazy (Unplugged)/ Crazy/ Say'n I Love U/ Girls of the world/ If Life is So Short/ If Life is So Short (Live)

ALSO APPEAR ON:

Bravo All-Stars—Let the Music Heal Your Soul *gil*— If You Only Knew (featuring the Moffatts) *Alabama Christmas, Volume II*—Christmas Love (the Moffatts provide background vocals)

Music from the Motion Picture Never Been Kissed

Semisonic, "Never You Mind"/ Willis, "Standing By"/ Jimmy Eat World, "Licky Denver Mint"/ Remy Zero, "Problem"/ The Cardigans, "Erase/Rewind"/ Kendall Payne, "Closer to Myself"/ R.E.M., "At My Most Beautiful"/ Block, "Catch a Falling Star"/ Swirl360, "Candy in the Sun"/ "Until You Loved Me"/ Ozomatli, "Cumbia de Los Muertos"/ John Lennon and Yoko Ono, "Watching the Wheels"/ The Smiths, "Please, Please, Please, Let Me Get What I Want"/ Sonichrome, "Innocent Journey"/ The Beach Boys, "Don't Worry Baby"/ Jeremy Jordan, "A Girl Named Happiness (Never Been Kissed)"

The Moffatts on the Web

With over one hundred and ninety sites to go at (and that's at the last count), there's plenty of Moffatt surfing to be done. Each of the guys has several fan shrines, as you'd expect, but the vast majority are about the band as a whole. So log on, and away we go....

www.themoffatts.com is the official Website. It has bios of the band, samples of songs from *all* their albums, as well as news and tour schedules updated very regulary. It's invaluable.

www.moffatthight.com is the Moffatts site at the Capitol Records site. You can read the record company bio, get updated on what's coming out, and plenty of other things. Also worth checking out from the record companies is *www.emiusic.ca* and *www.emimusic.de* (if you speak German).

Another site among the many that are well worth noting is The Ultimate Moffatts Home Page (*www.cleggo.net*). Most of the Websites are part of the Moffatts webring, which enables you to click directly from one site to the next.

You can also subscribe to a Moffatts online mailing list. Simply send an e-mail to listserv@home.ease./soft.com, leaving the subject line blank. In the body of the message, write SUBSCRIBE MOFFATTS-L and you'll start receiving hundreds of e-mails about the band . . . not bad, huh?

GET THE SIZZLING INSIDE STORY ON THE WORLD'S HOTTEST BAND!

BACKSTREET BOYS

They've Got it Goin' On!

Anna Louise Golden

Find out all about AJ, Brian, Howie, Kevin, and Nick step into their world, see what makes them tick, what kind of girls they like, how they make their way-cool music, and much, much more! Includes eight pages of cool color photos.

BACKSTREET BOYS
Anna Louise Golden
0-312-96853-1_____ $3.99 U.S. _____ $4.99 CAN.

Publishers Book and Audio Mailing Service
P.O. Box 070059, Staten Island, NY 10307
Please send me the book(s) I have checked above. I am enclosing $_____ (please add $1.50 for the first book, and $.50 for each additional book to cover postage and handling. Send check or money order only—no CODs or charge my VISA, MASTERCARD, DISCOVER or AMERICAN EXPRESS card.

Card Number_____
Expiration date_____Signature_____
Name_____
Address_____
City_____State/Zip_____
Please allow six weeks for delivery. Prices subject to change without notice. Payment in U.S. funds only. New York residents add applicable sales tax.

BOYS 10/98